1 The nature of economics

The economic problem

Economics is concerned with the ways by which societies organise productive resources in order to satisfy people's wants.

The two key terms in the above definition, **resources** and **wants**, are considered below.

Resources Revised

The resources of a country are referred to as **factors of production**. Four factors of production may be identified.

Land — includes all natural resources, raw materials, the fertility of the soil and resources found in the sea. Some resources are **renewable resources**, i.e. they can be replaced naturally after use (e.g. solar energy, wind power, wood, fish). Such resources are likely to be sustainable unless they are consumed more quickly than they can be replaced. Others are **non-renewable resources**, i.e. continued consumption will eventually result in their exhaustion.

Labour — refers to those people involved in the production of goods and services and includes all human effort both physical and mental.

Capital — any man-made aids to production, including factory buildings, offices, machinery and IT equipment, which are used to make other goods and services.

Enterprise — the entrepreneur performs two essential functions:
- bringing together the other factors of production so that goods and services can be produced and
- taking the risks involved in production

> **Factors of production** are resources and include land, labour, capital and enterprise.
>
> **Renewable resources** are those resources whose stock levels can be maintained at a certain level.
>
> **Non-renewable resources** are those resources which will eventually be completely depleted.
>
> **Capital** comprises man-made assets which can be used for production.

> **Typical mistake**
>
> Describing money as capital — you should avoid this. As a factor of production, capital is something tangible which is used to make other goods.

Now test yourself Tested

1 Identify the factor of production in each of the following cases:
   (a) Copper deposits in Zambia.
   (b) A woman who opens a hairdressing salon.
   (c) Machinery used in car production.
   (d) An engineer making computer games for a company.

Answer on p. 103

Scarcity and choice

All societies face the problem that wants are infinite but resources are limited in supply. This is the underlying reason for the fundamental economic problem of **scarcity**. The issue of scarcity means that societies face a series of questions and that a number of choices have to be made.

> **Scarcity** exists because resources are finite whereas wants are infinite.

1 What to produce and how much to produce?

Goods produced are usually classified into consumer goods and services and capital goods and services:

● **Consumer goods** are those which give satisfaction (or utility) to consumers (e.g. iphones, curry or cars). Similarly, **consumer services** give satisfaction or utility (e.g. car repairs, IT services or foreign holidays).

● **Capital goods** are those required to produce other goods — both other capital goods and consumer goods. Examples include machinery and factory buildings. Examples of **capital services** include machinery repair companies and finance companies offering loans to businesses.

2 How should goods and services be produced?

Production may be **labour intensive**, i.e. a high proportion of labour used relative to capital, or **capital intensive**, i.e. a high proportion of capital used relative to labour.

> **Examiner's tip**
>
> To avoid confusion between capital goods and consumer goods, consider how they are used: anything which is an aid to production is classified as a capital good whereas anything used by someone for final consumption is classified as a consumer good.

3 How should the goods produced be allocated?

This choice is concerned with the distribution of the goods produced and will affect the degree of **equality** in the society.

Countries may approach an answer to these questions in different ways. The two extreme forms are:

● **The free market economy** — where answers to the above questions are determined by market forces.

● **The command or centrally planned economy** — where answers to the above questions are determined by the state.

In practice, all economies are **mixed economies** — i.e. a mixture of the free market economy and the command economy. What differs between countries is the degree of that mix. The free market and mixed economy are discussed in the next chapter.

> **Now test yourself**
>
> 2 Classify the following into capital and consumer goods:
> (a) A laptop used by a company director for his business.
> (b) A curry eaten by Marie for her lunch.
> (c) A visit to a spa by Kirsten.
> (d) A car used to transport a manager between offices.
>
> Answer on p. 103
>
> Tested

Specialisation and the division of labour

Division of labour occurs when workers specialise in very specific tasks — i.e. the work is divided up into many smaller parts so that each worker is responsible for a very small part of the product or service being provided.

> **Division of labour** occurs when the work is split up into small tasks.

my **revisi⏻n** notes

EDEXCEL **AS**
ECONOMICS

Quintin Brewer
Rachel Cole

HODDER
EDUCATION

Hodder Education, an Hachette UK company, 338 Euston Road, London NW1 3BH

Orders

Bookpoint Ltd, 130 Milton Park, Abingdon, Oxfordshire OX14 4SB

tel: 01235 827827

fax: 01235 400401

e-mail: education@bookpoint.co.uk

Lines are open 9.00 a.m.–5.00 p.m., Monday to Saturday, with a 24-hour message answering service. You can also order through the Hodder Education website: www.hoddereducation.co.uk

ISBN 978-1-4441-7979-8

First printed 2013

Impression number 5 4 3 2

Year 2017 2016 2015 2014

Cover photo reproduced by permission of Tomislav Forgo/Fotolia

Typeset by Datapage (India) Pvt. Ltd.
Printed in Spain

Hachette UK's policy is to use papers that are natural, renewable and recyclable products and made from wood grown in sustainable forests. The logging and manufacturing processes are expected to conform to the environmental regulations of the country of origin.

P2184

Get the most from this book

Everyone has to decide his or her own revision strategy, but it is essential to review your work, learn it and test your understanding. These Revision Notes will help you to do that in a planned way, topic by topic. Use this book as the cornerstone of your revision and don't hesitate to write in it — personalise your notes and check your progress by ticking off each section as you revise.

☑ **Tick to track your progress**

Use the revision planner on pages 4 and 5 to plan your revision, topic by topic. Tick each box when you have:

● revised and understood a topic

● tested yourself

● practised the exam questions and gone online to check your answers and complete the quick quizzes

You can also keep track of your revision by ticking off each topic heading in the book. You may find it helpful to add your own notes as you work through each topic.

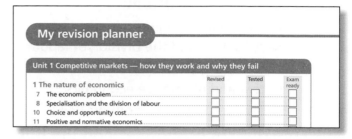

Features to help you succeed

Examiner's tips and summaries

Expert tips are given throughout the book to help you polish your exam technique in order to maximise your chances in the exam.

The summaries provide a quick-check bullet list for each topic.

Typical mistake

The authors identify the typical mistakes candidates make and explain how you can avoid them.

Definitions and key words

Clear, concise definitions of essential key terms are provided on the page where they appear.

Key words from the specification are highlighted in bold for you throughout the book.

Exam practice

Practice exam questions are provided for each topic. Use them to consolidate your revision and practise your exam skills.

Now test yourself

These short, knowledge-based questions provide the first step in testing your learning. Answers are at the back of the book.

Revision activities

These activities will help you to understand each topic in an interactive way.

Online

Go online to check your answers to the exam questions and try out the extra quick quizzes at **www.hodderplus.co.uk/myrevisionnotes**

My revision planner

Exam practice answers and quick quizzes at **www.hodderplus.co.uk/myrevisionnotes**

Unit 2 Managing the economy

Countdown to my exams

6–8 weeks to go

- Start by looking at the specification — make sure you know exactly what material you need to revise and the style of the examination. Use the revision planner on pages 4 and 5 to familiarise yourself with the topics.
- Organise your notes, making sure you have covered everything on the specification. The revision planner will help you to group your notes into topics.
- Work out a realistic revision plan that will allow you time for relaxation. Set aside days and times for all the subjects that you need to study, and stick to your timetable.
- Set yourself sensible targets. Break your revision down into focused sessions of around 40 minutes, divided by breaks. These Revision Notes organise the basic facts into short, memorable sections to make revising easier.

Revised ☐

4–6 weeks to go

- Read through the relevant sections of this book and refer to the examiner's tips, examiner's summaries, typical mistakes and key terms. Tick off the topics as you feel confident about them. Highlight those topics you find difficult and look at them again in detail.
- Test your understanding of each topic by working through the 'Now test yourself' questions and 'Revision activities' in the book. Look up the answers at the back of the book.
- Make a note of any problem areas as you revise, and ask your teacher to go over these in class.
- Look at past papers. They are one of the best ways to revise and practise your exam skills. Write or prepare planned answers to the exam practice questions provided in this book. Check your answers online and try out the extra quick quizzes at **www.hodderplus.co.uk/ myrevisionnotes**
- Use the revision activities to try different revision methods. For example, you can make notes using mind maps, spider diagrams or flash cards.
- Track your progress using the revision planner and give yourself a reward when you have achieved your target.

Revised ☐

One week to go

- Try to fit in at least one more timed practice of an entire past paper and seek feedback from your teacher, comparing your work closely with the mark scheme.
- Check the revision planner to make sure you haven't missed out any topics. Brush up on any areas of difficulty by talking them over with a friend or getting help from your teacher.
- Attend any revision classes put on by your teacher. Remember, he or she is an expert at preparing people for examinations.

Revised ☐

The day before the examination

- Flick through these Revision Notes for useful reminders, for example the examiner's tips, examiner's summaries, typical mistakes and key terms.
- Check the time and place of your examination.
- Make sure you have everything you need — extra pens and pencils, tissues, a watch, bottled water, sweets.
- Allow some time to relax and have an early night to ensure you are fresh and alert for the examination.

Revised ☐

My exams

AS Economics Unit 1

Date: . . . .

Time: . . . .

Location:. . . . .

AS Economics Unit 2

Date: . . . .

Time: . . . .

Location:. . . . .

Advantages

Revised

The following factors help to explain why the division of labour has been widely adopted.

- Each worker specialises in tasks for which he or she is best suited.
- Therefore, he or she only has to be trained in one task.
- Less time is wasted because a worker no longer has to move from one task to another.
- In manufacturing such an approach enables production line methods to be employed and allows an increased use of machinery.
- In turn, this helps to increase productivity and to reduce average costs of production.

> **Typical mistake**
>
> Thinking that division of labour entails increased training costs. In practice, training costs should be reduced because the worker only has to be trained in one particular task.

Disadvantages

Revised

Despite the above advantages, certain problems are associated with the division of labour including:

- Monotony and boredom for workers: this could result in a decrease in productivity.
- Loss of skills: workers trained in one particular task have only limited skills. This could be a problem if they are made redundant.
- A strike by one group of workers could bring the entire production facility to a standstill.
- There is a lack of variety because all goods produced on a production line are identical.

Limits to the division of labour

Revised

Certain factors will limit the extent to which the division of labour can be applied.

- The size of the market: if there is only a small market then it will be more difficult to specialise.
- The type of the product: for example, designer fashion products are likely to be unique and not suitable for division of labour.
- Transport costs: if these are very high then large-scale production and the division of labour may not be possible.

Now test yourself

Tested

3 Which one of the following would make it more difficult for a firm to adopt a greater degree of specialisation?
   (a) Increasing sales.
   (b) New machinery available.
   (c) Falling costs of transporting goods to consumers.
   (d) Production of unique products which are designed to meet individual consumer wishes.

Answer on p. 103

Choice and opportunity cost

Scarcity implies that choices must be made. However, each choice involves an **opportunity cost**. If a country's resources are used to manufacture one product, then it must forgo an alternative product which could have been produced with those resources. The next best alternative forgone is called the opportunity cost of what has been produced.

> **Opportunity cost** is the next best alternative which is forgone when a choice is made.

Opportunity cost
`Revised`

Opportunity cost, therefore, is a **real cost** measured in terms of something that is forgone.

Examples of opportunity cost include:

- For a government: suppose it has £10 million with which to fund one of its two main priorities, both requiring a £10 million investment — building a new hospital or building a new university. If it decides that its first preference is the hospital while the second preference is the university, then the opportunity cost of building the hospital will be building the university.

- For a firm: it might have to make a choice between two priorities — buying a new IT system and building a new factory. If it chooses the IT system then the opportunity cost is the new factory.

- For a consumer: a woman might have enough money to buy either an ebook or an itune. If she decides to buy the ebook then the opportunity cost is the itune.

> **Typical mistake**
>
> Considering opportunity cost in terms of money. This is incorrect: opportunity cost must be measured as a real cost — i.e. in terms of goods forgone when a choice is made.

Now test yourself
`Tested`

4 Why do societies have to make choices about what to produce?

5 If a person's top two priorities are a holiday in Greece and a new home cinema system but there is only enough money for one of these, then what would be the opportunity cost of purchasing the home cinema system?

Answers on p. 103

Economic goods and free goods
`Revised`

Economic goods are created from resources which are limited in supply and so are scarce. Consequently, they command a price.

Free goods are unlimited in supply, such as sunlight or sand on a beach. Consumption by one person does not limit consumption by others. Therefore, the opportunity cost of consuming a free good is zero.

Now test yourself

6 Why does the consumption of free goods not incur an opportunity cost?

Answer on p. 103
`Tested`

Positive and normative economics

Positive economic statements

Revised

Positive economic statements are based on facts that can be proved or disproved. They include what was, is or will be and these statements can be verified as being true or false by reference to the data or by using a scientific approach.

Economists often use 'models' as a way of predicting behaviour. It is possible to make positive statements on the basis of models, such as the impact on price of a product following an increase in demand.

> **Positive economic statements** are objective statements based on evidence or facts which can, therefore, be proved or disproved.

Normative economic statements

Revised

Normative economic statements are based on value judgements and are, therefore, subjective. They relate to what:

- might be good or bad, or
- should be or ought to be, or
- would be fair or unfair

Normative economics is usually associated with economic policy. In this unit, for example, it is concerned with issues such as whether or not there should be:

- a minimum price for alcohol
- subsidies for green energy (e.g. wind farms)
- road tolls
- an increase in the tax on cigarettes
- more private sector provision in the health service

> **Normative economic statements** are subjective statements based on value judgements and cannot be proved or disproved.

> **Typical mistake**
>
> Answers relating to normative statements often refer to these statements as opinions. Although this is not technically incorrect, it is much better to use the term 'value judgement' or 'subjective view' to describe them.

> **Now test yourself**
>
> Tested
>
> 7 Which of the following are positive statements and which are normative statements?
>
> (a) Taxes on the bankers should be increased.
>
> (b) The UK experienced a double dip recession in 2011–12.
>
> (c) New technology has caused a fall in the price of mobile phones.
>
> (d) High food prices are unfair on the poor.
>
> Answers on p. 103

Production possibility frontiers (PPFs)

A **production possibility frontier** shows combinations of two goods which could be produced by an economy if all its resources and employed fully and efficiently. Figure 1.1 shows a PPF.

> A **production possibility frontier** illustrates the maximum potential output of an economy when all resources are fully employed.

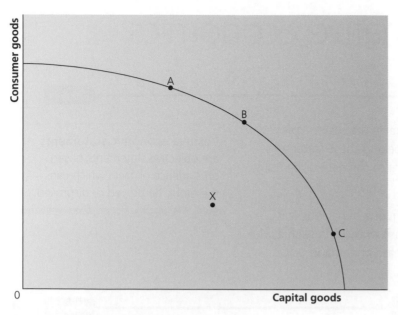

Figure 1.1 A production possibility frontier (PPF)

By definition, any point on the PPF (e.g. A, B or C) implies that all resources are fully employed. However, if an economy is operating at point X it would indicate that there are unemployed resources in that economy (e.g. some workers may be unemployed or machinery may be unused).

PPFs and opportunity cost

Revised

- The PPF is drawn as a curve in Figure 1.1.
- This indicates the principle of increasing opportunity costs — as the output of capital goods is increased, more and more consumer goods must be sacrificed.
- In Figure 1.2, an increase in output of capital goods from 0M to 0S means that output of consumer goods falls from 0L to 0R.
- A further increase in output of capital goods from 0S to 0V causes a larger fall in output of consumer goods from 0R to 0T.

Examiner's tip

If the PPF was a straight line, the opportunity cost would be constant.

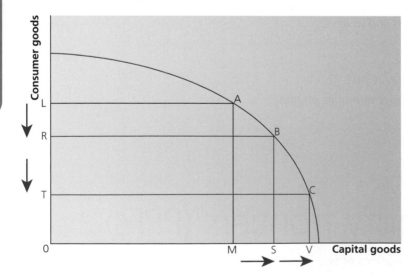

Figure 1.2 Production possibility frontiers and opportunity cost

Exam practice answers and quick quizzes at **www.hodderplus.co.uk/myrevisionnotes**

PPFs and economic growth

PPFs may be used to illustrate **economic growth**.

- Look at Figure 1.2. Suppose that the economy is currently operating at point A on the PPF with 0L consumer goods and 0M capital goods being produced.

- It is also assumed that the 0M capital goods produced are just sufficient to replace worn-out machinery.

- If there is a reallocation of resources so that the production of capital goods is increased to 0S, then only 0R consumer goods can now be produced.

- Therefore the opportunity cost of producing MS more capital goods is LR consumer goods.

This reduction in the output of consumer goods implies a fall in current living standards. However, in the long run there will be economic growth because the extra capital goods will cause an increase in the productive capacity of the economy, resulting in a rightward shift in the PPF as shown below:

> **Economic growth** refers to an increase in the productive capacity of the economy which indicates that real incomes have increased.

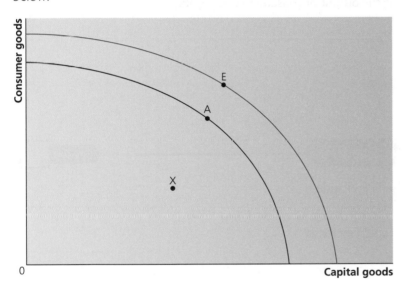

Figure 1.3 Production possibility frontiers and economic growth

It can be seen that if the economy moved from point A to point E then more of both capital goods and consumer goods could be produced. In turn, this implies that living standards would increase in the long run.

> **Typical mistake**
>
> Students often confuse an increased utilisation of resources with economic growth. Therefore, a movement from point X to point A is *not* economic growth; it just represents the use of unemployed resources. However, a movement from point A to point E is economic growth because there is an increase in productive capacity associated with a rightward shift of the PPF.

8 With reference to the diagram below:

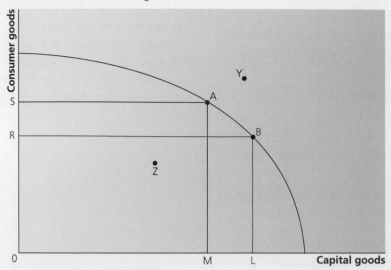

(a) What does point Z represent?

(b) Under what circumstances could the combination of goods at point Y be achieved?

(c) What is the opportunity cost of increasing the output of consumer goods by RS?

(d) How might this affect:

   (i) present living standards, and

   (ii) future living standards?

Answers on p. 103

Factors causing an outward shift in the PPF   Revised

Factors which might cause an outward shift in the PPF include:

- Discovery of new natural resources (e.g. oil).
- Development of new methods of production which increase productivity.
- Advances in technology.
- Improvements in education and training which increase the productivity of the workforce.
- Factors which lead to an increase in the size of the workforce (e.g. immigration; an increase in the retirement age; better childcare enabling more women to join the workforce).

Factors causing an inward shift in the PPF   Revised

Factors which might cause an inward shift in the PPF include:

- Natural disasters (e.g. earthquakes; floods which cause a destruction of productive capacity).
- Depletion of natural resources.
- Factors causing a reduction in the size of the workforce (e.g. emigration; increase in number of years spent in compulsory education).
- A deep recession which results in a loss of productive capacity, with factories closing down permanently.

Examiner's tip

Remember that the PPF represents the possible outputs of two goods which could potentially be produced. Points on the PPF do not represent what is actually produced unless all resources are fully employed.

Now test yourself — Tested

9 What will be the effect on a PPF of each of the following?

   (a) Improvements in education and training leading to an increase in labour productivity.

   (b) A tsunami in Japan causes the closure of nuclear power stations.

   (c) An increase in the amount of capital per worker.

   (d) An increase in immigration of people aged between 16 and 65.

Answers on p. 103

Exam practice

Demand for healthcare has been rising rapidly because of an ageing population, new medical discoveries, advances in medical technology and rising staff costs. Despite a very significant increase in spending during the period 2000 to 2010, there is still evidence of shortages of hospital beds and waiting lists are increasing. In the next few years it is likely that demand for healthcare will greatly outpace the supply of healthcare services. Meanwhile, the government is committed to a massive increase in foreign aid.

(a) How does the extract illustrate the fundamental economic problem? [4]

(b) Using examples, explain the opportunity cost of an increase in government expenditure on foreign aid. [4]

(c) Assess the effect on the production possibility curve of a reduction in government spending on the NHS. Illustrate your answer with a diagram. [10]

Answers and quick quizzes online

Online

Examiner's summary

You should have an understanding of:

✔ What the term 'economics' covers.

✔ The four key factors of production: land, labour, capital and enterprise.

✔ The meaning of scarcity and the need to make choices.

✔ The difference between consumer goods and services and capital goods and services.

✔ The difference between labour intensive production and capital intensive production.

✔ Opportunity cost and its significance for individuals, firms and the government.

✔ The distinction between free goods and economic goods.

✔ Positive and normative economic statements.

✔ Production possibility frontiers including the ability to draw them accurately.

✔ The use of PPFs to illustrate opportunity cost and economic growth.

✔ Factors which can cause an inward or outward shift in the PPF.

✔ The meaning of specialisation and the division of labour.

✔ Advantages and disadvantages of the division of labour.

2 Free market economies and the price mechanism

Free market economies

A **free market economy** is one in which resources are allocated by the price mechanism. The main characteristics of a free market economy may be summarised as follows:

- private ownership of resources
- market forces — i.e. supply and demand — determine prices
- producers aim to maximise profits
- consumers aim to maximise satisfaction
- resources are allocated by the price mechanism

> A **free market economy** refers to an economy in which the market forces of supply and demand determine how resources are allocated.

> **Typical mistake**
>
> Assuming that there is government intervention in a free market economy.

> **Now test yourself**   Tested ☐
>
> 1   Identify four characteristics of a free market economy.
>
> **Answer on p. 103**

Advantages   Revised ☐

Advantages of a free market economy include:

- **Consumer sovereignty** — this implies that spending decisions by consumers determine what is produced.
- **Flexibility** — the free market system can respond quickly to changes in consumer wants.
- **No officials** are needed to allocate resources.
- **Profit motive** — provides an incentive for firms to take risks.
- **Competition** and the profit motive help to promote an efficient allocation of resources.
- **Increased choice** for consumers compared with a command economy.
- **Economic and political freedom** for consumers and producers — to own resources.

> **Now test yourself**
>
> 2   What is meant by 'consumer sovereignty'?
> 3   Outline three other advantages of a free market economy.
>
> **Answers on p. 103**
>
> Tested ☐

Disadvantages   Revised ☐

Various problems are associated with free market economies:

- **Inequality** — those who own resources are likely to become richer than those who do not own resources.
- **Trade cycles** — free market economies may suffer from instability in the form of booms and slumps.

Exam practice answers and quick quizzes at **www.hodderplus.co.uk/myrevisionnotes**

- **Imperfect information** — consumers may be unable to make rational choices if they have inadequate information or if there is asymmetric information (see chapter 5).
- **Monopolies** — there is a danger that a firm may become the sole supplier of a product and then exploit consumers by charging prices higher than the free market equilibrium.
- **Externalities** — these are costs and benefits which are not taken into account when goods are produced and consumed.

To overcome the types of problem associated with free market economies state intervention is usually required. Once there is state intervention in the economy, it will be regarded as a **mixed economy**.

In practice, there are no absolutely free market economies: most are mixed economies. In these economies, some resources are allocated by the price mechanism while others are allocated by the state.

> A **mixed economy** is a combination of a free market economy and a command economy.

> **Revision activity**
> - Make a list of the characteristics of a mixed economy.
> - Draw up a list of the advantages and disadvantages of a mixed economy.

> **Examiner's tip**
> When thinking about the advantages and disadvantages of a free market economy, consider the impact on individuals, businesses and the whole economy.

Now test yourself   Tested ☐

4 Why does inequality occur in a free market economy?

5 Outline three other disadvantages of a free market economy.

Answers on p. 103

The demand curve

Demand refers to the amount demanded by consumers at given prices over a certain period of time. It is important to include a reference to prices and to the time period in a definition of demand.

Demand is not the same as 'want' — 'wanting' a product which cannot be afforded is not demand. Demand must include the ability to pay for the product or service.

> **Demand** refers to the amount demanded by consumers at each price over a certain period of time.

> **Typical mistake**
> Confusing 'want' with 'demand': wants refer to desires, and desires may be unaffordable, whereas demand is backed by money.

Shape of the demand curve   Revised ☐

Figure 2.1 shows that the demand curve is downward sloping from left to right, indicating that more will be demanded as price falls.

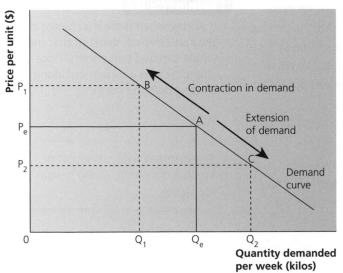

Figure 2.1 Movements along a demand curve

The demand curve demonstrates how a fall in price will cause an increase in the quantity demanded (or an extension in demand) and a rise in price will cause a decrease in quantity demanded (or contraction in demand).

This is based on:

- **The substitution effect** — when there is a rise in price the consumer (whose income has remained the same) will tend to buy more of a relatively lower-priced good and less of a higher-priced one.
- **The income effect** — this is the effect of a change in real income on the quantity demanded, with relative prices unchanged.

Now test yourself

6   Define the term 'demand'.

Answer on p. 103

Tested

Revision activity

Construct a demand curve on graph paper based on the following information:

Price per kilo ($)	Quantity of soya demanded per week (kilos)
10	100 000
9	120 000
8	140 000
7	160 000
6	180 000
5	200 000

Shifts in the demand curve

Revised

Various factors can cause a shift in the whole demand curve. These include changes in:

- **Real incomes.** An increase in real incomes implies that incomes (after discounting the effects of inflation) have increased. This would result in an increase in demand for most goods and services, causing a rightward shift in the demand curve.
- **Size or age distribution of the population.** An increase in the size of the population will cause an increase in demand for most goods and services.
- **Tastes, fashions or preferences.** For example, a decrease in the popularity of cabbage will cause a leftward shift in its demand curve.
- **Prices of substitutes or complements.** If there is a change in the price of a related good, it will affect the demand curve for the product (e.g. if the price of beef rises then the demand for a substitute, such as lamb, will increase). In contrast, if there is a rise in the price of petrol (a complement to cars) then the demand curve for cars would shift to the left.
- **The amount of advertising or promotion.** A successful advertising campaign would cause an increase in demand.
- **Interest rates** affect the cost of borrowing money. For example, an increase in interest rates increases the cost of borrowing money for mortgages, so causing a decrease in demand for houses.

Examiner's tip

It is only when there is a change in the conditions of demand that the whole demand curve shifts. Price changes cause a movement along an existing demand curve.

The **interest rate** is the cost of credit (borrowing), or the reward for saving.

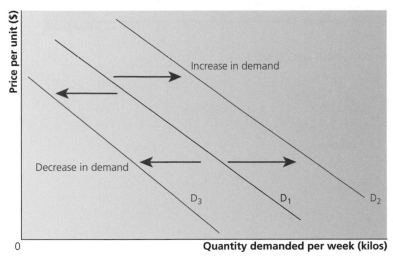

Figure 2.2 Shifts in the demand curve

Figure 2.2 illustrates how an increase in demand would cause the whole demand curve to shift to the right whereas a decrease in demand would cause the whole demand curve to shift to the left.

Revision activity

Suppose an increase in the size of the population causes an increase in the demand for soya. Construct a new demand curve on your previous graph based on the following information:

Price per kilo ($)	Old quantity of soya demanded per week (kilos)	New quantity of soya demanded per week (kilos)
10	100 000	120 000
9	120 000	140 000
8	140 000	160 000
7	160 000	180 000
6	180 000	200 000
5	200 000	220 000

Now test yourself

Tested ☐

7 What would be the effect of the following on the demand for houses in the UK?

   (a) An increase in immigration into the UK.

   (b) A decrease in real incomes.

   (c) An increase in the price of rented accommodation.

   (d) A rise in mortgage interest rates.

Answer on p. 103

The supply curve

Supply refers to the amount supplied by producers at given prices over a certain period of time. As with demand, it is important to include a reference to prices and to the time period in the definition.

> **Supply** refers to how much is supplied at each price over a certain period of time.

Shape of the supply curve

Figure 2.3 shows that the supply curve is upward sloping from left to right, indicating that more will be supplied as price increases.

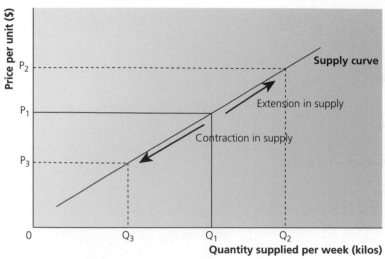

Figure 2.3 Movements along a supply curve

When the price rises it becomes more profitable for producers to supply a product and so they have an incentive to increase production. In contrast, when there is a fall in price it becomes less profitable to supply a product and so firms will reduce output and/or exit the market.

Therefore:

● a rise in price will cause an increase in the quantity supplied (or an extension in supply) and

● a fall in price will cause a decrease in quantity supplied (or contraction in supply).

Revision activity

Construct a supply curve on graph paper based on the following information:

Price per kilo ($)	Quantity of soya supplied per week (kilos)
10	200 000
9	180 000
8	160 000
7	140 000
6	120 000
5	100 000

Now test yourself

Tested

8　Define the term 'supply'.

Answer on p. 103

Shifts in the supply curve

Various factors will cause a shift in the whole supply curve. These include changes in:

- **Costs of production** — these include wages, raw materials, energy and rent. An increase in costs of production (e.g. electricity prices) would cause the whole supply curve to shift to the left.
- **Productivity of the workforce** — labour productivity refers to the output per worker per hour worked. If there was a rise in productivity then the whole supply curve would shift to the right.
- **Indirect taxes** — an indirect tax raises the cost of supply and so causes the supply curve to shift to the left. A rise in VAT will cause the supply curve to become steeper because it is a percentage of the price of a product, whereas a rise in a specific tax (e.g. 20p per unit) would cause a parallel leftward shift in the supply curve.
- **Subsidies** — these are grants to producers from the government which effectively lead to a reduction in costs of production, causing a rightward shift in the supply curve.
- **Technology** — new inventions and new technology usually result in an increase in productivity, causing the supply curve to shift to the right.
- **Discoveries of new reserves of a raw material** — if for example a country discovers new oil reserves, the supply curve will shift to the right.

Figure 2.4 illustrates that an increase in supply would cause the whole supply curve to shift to the right, whereas a decrease in supply would cause the whole supply curve to shift to the left.

> **Examiner's tip**
>
> It is only when there is a change in the conditions of supply that the whole supply curve shifts. Price changes cause a movement along an existing supply curve.

> **Typical mistake**
>
> Showing an increase in supply as an upward (leftward) shift. Remember that an increase in supply will cause the supply curve to shift to the right.

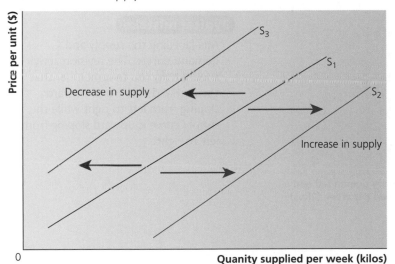

Figure 2.4 Shifts of a supply curve

Revision activity

Assume there is a good soya harvest. Construct a new supply curve on your previous graph based on the following information:

Price per kilo ($)	Old quantity of soya supplied per week (kilos)	New quantity of soya supplied per week (kilos)
10	200 000	220 000
9	180 000	200 000
8	160 000	180 000
7	140 000	160 000
6	120 000	140 000
5	100 000	120 000

Now test yourself
Tested

9   What would be the effect of the following on the supply of tea?

(a) A subsidy to tea producers.

(b) An increase in wages of tea plantation workers.

(c) An increase in productivity of tea workers.

(d) A drought in tea growing regions.

Answer on p. 103

Market equilibrium

The meaning of market equilibrium
Revised

The **equilibrium** price and output are determined by the interaction of supply and demand (see Figure 2.5).

When the quantity supplied is equal to the quantity demanded of a particular product, equilibrium is said to exist. The equilibrium price and output will not change unless one of the conditions of supply or conditions of demand change.

The **equilibrium (price and quantity)** is determined by the interaction of the supply and demand curves. The equilibrium price and quantity would not change unless there was a change in the conditions of demand or supply.

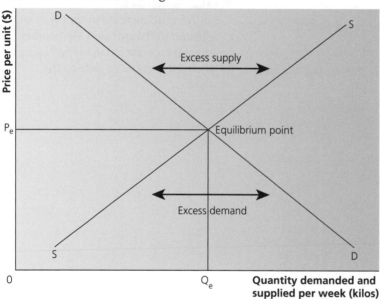

Figure 2.5 Equilibrium price and quantity

> **Typical mistake**
>
> Mis-labelling the supply and demand curves. The revision activity should help you to remember that the demand curve is downward sloping from left to right while the supply curve is upward sloping from left to right.

Revision activity

Construct a demand curve and a supply curve on graph paper based on the following information:

Price per kilo ($)	Quantity of soya demanded per week (kilos)	Quantity of soya supplied per week (kilos)
10	100 000	200 000
9	120 000	180 000
8	140 000	160 000
7	160 000	140 000
6	180 000	120 000
5	200 000	100 000

Find the equilibrium point and show the equilibrium price and quantity on your diagram.

Exam practice answers and quick quizzes at **www.hodderplus.co.uk/myrevisionnotes**

Functions of price

Revised

The key functions of the price mechanism in a free market economy are:

- **As a rationing device** — market forces will ensure that the amount demanded is exactly equal to the amount supplied.
- To determine **changes in wants** — a change in demand will be reflected in a change in price.
- As a **signalling device** — to producers to increase or decrease the amount supplied.
- As **an incentive** — the prospect of making a profit acts as an incentive to firms to produce goods and services.

> **Typical mistake**
>
> Assuming that the function of a free market economy is to keep prices stable. While it is true that the forces of supply and demand (market forces) help to determine the equilibrium price, any change in the conditions of supply and demand will cause the equilibrium price to change.

Excess demand and excess supply

Revised

Figure 2.6 illustrates what happens if the price is not currently at its equilibrium level.

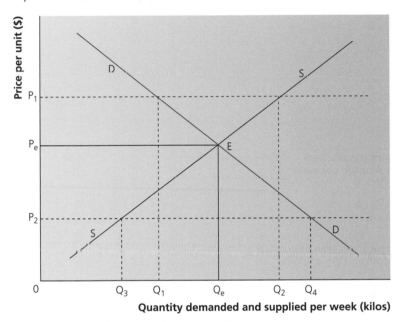

Figure 2.6 Excess demand and excess supply

If the price is above the equilibrium price of P_e then there will be **excess supply**. For example, if the price is at P_1 then the quantity demanded will be only Q_1 while the quantity supplied will be Q_2, so there will be a surplus of Q_1Q_2.

Market forces will cause price to fall to P_e which will lead to an extension of demand and a contraction in supply, so eliminating the excess supply.

If the price is below the equilibrium price of P_e then there will be **excess demand**. For example, if the price is at P_2 then the quantity demanded will be Q_4 while the quantity supplied will be only Q_3, so there will be a shortage of Q_3Q_4.

Market forces will cause the price to rise to P_e which will lead to an extension of supply and a contraction in demand, so eliminating the excess demand.

> **Excess supply** implies that the quantity supplied is greater than the quantity demanded at the existing price.
>
> **Excess demand** implies that the quantity demanded is greater than the quantity supplied at the existing price.

> **Now test yourself**
>
> 10 If the current price is above the free market price, identify whether there is excess supply or excess demand.
>
> 11 If the existing market price is above the equilibrium price, explain how equilibrium is restored.
>
> Answers on p. 104
>
> Tested

Changes in the equilibrium price

A change in the equilibrium price can be caused by:

- a change in the conditions of demand (which would cause the demand curve to shift) or
- a change in the conditions of supply (which would cause the supply curve to shift).

An increase in demand

This would cause a rightward shift in the demand curve, a rise in price and an increase in the quantity as shown in Figure 2.7.

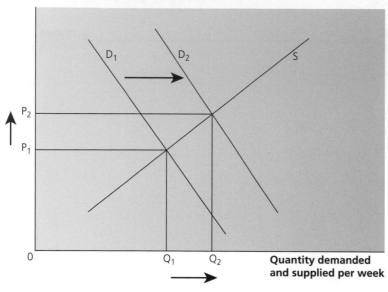

Figure 2.7 Increase in demand

> **Examiner's tip**
>
> Before considering any change in equilibrium price and quantity, you should always begin with a diagram like Figure 2.5, showing the initial equilibrium price and output.

A decrease in demand

This would cause a leftward shift in the demand curve, a fall in price and a decrease in the quantity as shown in Figure 2.8.

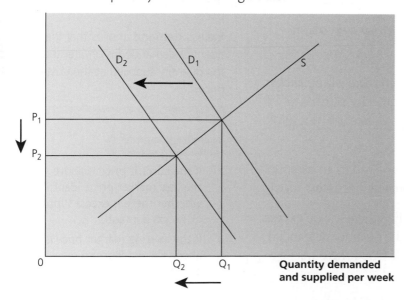

Figure 2.8 Decrease in demand

Exam practice answers and quick quizzes at **www.hodderplus.co.uk/myrevisionnotes**

An increase in supply

This would cause a rightward shift in the supply curve, a fall in price and an increase in the quantity as shown in Figure 2.9.

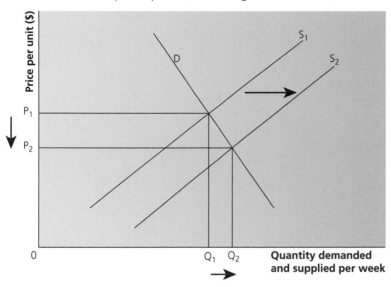

Figure 2.9 Increase in supply

A decrease in supply

This would cause a leftward shift in the supply curve, a rise in price and a decrease in the quantity as shown in Figure 2.10.

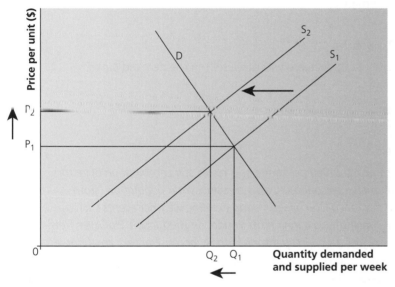

Figure 2.10 Decrease in supply

Now test yourself   Tested ☐

12 For each of the following, explain what happens to the equilibrium price and quantity. (You might find it helpful to sketch supply and demand diagrams.)

  (a) Effect on beef of a rise in the cost of animal feed.

  (b) A change in tastes in favour of blueberries.

  (c) An increase in the productivity of workers harvesting rice.

  (d) A health scare relating to bananas.

Answer on p. 104

Exam practice

1 Which of the following is a function of the price mechanism?

   A To stabilise prices.

   B To maintain the equilibrium price.

   C To ration out scarce goods.

   D To equalise the distribution of income.   [1+3]

2 The demand curve for iPads will shift to the right if there is:

   A An increase in costs of production.

   B A rise in VAT on iPads.

   C An increase in the productivity of workers producing iPads.

   D An increase in real incomes of consumers.   [1+3]

3 The supply curve of potatoes will shift to the left if:

   A The cost of fertiliser increases.

   B There is an increase in advertising of potatoes.

   C New machinery enables more potatoes to be produced per acre.

   D The price of rice, a substitute for potatoes, increases in price.   [1+3]

4 *Statement 1: 'Annual increases in child benefit are linked to the rate of inflation.'*

   Statement 2: 'Only those people on low incomes should receive child benefit.'

   Which of the following best describes the two statements above?

   A Both statements are positive.

   B Statement 1 is positive and statement 2 is normative.

   C Both statements are normative.

   D Statement 1 is normative and statement 2 is positive.   [1+3]

5 Which of the following would cause the price of tea to decrease without a shift in the demand curve?

   A A decrease in the price of coffee.

   B An increase in the productivity of tea pickers.

   C An increase in the wages of tea pickers.

   D A decrease in real incomes of tea consumers.   [1+3]

6 *The price of rice rose significantly during 2008 to nearly $1000 per tonne as a result of a combination of factors including rising real incomes in developing and emerging economies; an increasing world population (from 6 billion in 1999 to 7 billion in 2011, expected to rise to 9 billion by 2025); and extreme weather events such as droughts, floods and hurricanes. Climate change might have a long-term impact on production. However, from 2009 until 2012 the price fell back to an average of just over $600 per tonne largely because of very good harvests.*

   (a) Illustrating your answer with a diagram, explain why the price of rice fell from nearly $1000 per tonne in 2008 to an average of just over $600 per tonne in the next four years.   [6]

   (b) Assess reasons why the price of rice might be expected to rise in the future. Include an appropriate supply and demand diagram.   [10]

Answers and quick quizzes online

Online

Examiner's summary

You should have an understanding of:

✔ The characteristics of a free market economy.

✔ The advantages and disadvantages of a free market economy.

✔ The reasons why there are mixed economies.

✔ How a price change causes a movement along a demand curve.

✔ How changes in the conditions of demand cause shifts in the demand curve.

✔ How a price change causes a movement along a supply curve.

✔ How changes in the conditions of supply cause shifts in the demand curve.

✔ How the equilibrium price and output is determined.

✔ How market forces will eliminate excess demand and excess supply.

✔ How changes in the conditions of demand and/or the conditions of supply would cause a change in the equilibrium price and quantity.

3 Elasticities

Price elasticity of demand (PED)

Price elasticity of demand is a measure of the responsiveness of the quantity demanded of a product to a change in its price.

> **Price elasticity of demand** measures the sensitivity of the quantity demanded of a product to a change in its own price.

Revised ☐

Measuring price elasticity of demand

$$PED = \frac{\text{percentage change in quantity demanded}}{\text{percentage change in price}}$$

> **Examiner's tip**
>
> To calculate a percentage change in, say, quantity demanded, it is necessary to divide the change in quantity demanded by the original quantity demanded and multiply the result by 100.

Interpreting results

PED will always have a negative value because price and quantity move in opposite directions (since the demand curve is downward sloping). In practice, the sign is usually ignored.

> **Typical mistake**
>
> Calculating PED using absolute changes rather than percentage changes.

Examples

(1) Price inelastic demand

Suppose a 100% increase in the price of oil led to a 20% fall in quantity demanded, then

$$PED \text{ would be } \frac{-20}{100} = -0.2$$

Demand is said to be price inelastic because a change in price has led to a smaller percentage change in quantity demanded.

When demand is price inelastic, the value of PED will be between 0 and 1.

(2) Price elastic demand

Suppose a 5% decrease in the price of a package holiday to Florida led to a 20% increase in quantity demanded, then

$$PED \text{ would be } \frac{+20}{-5} = -4.0$$

Demand is said to be price elastic because a change in price has led to a larger percentage change in quantity demanded.

When demand is price elastic, the value of PED will be greater than 1.

Figures 3.1a and 3.1b illustrate an inelastic and an elastic segment of a demand curve.

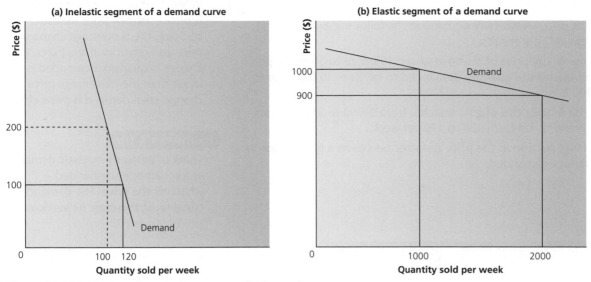

Figure 3.1 An inelastic and an elastic segment of a demand curve

(3) Unit elastic demand

Suppose a 15% decrease in the price of a digital camera to led to a 15% increase in quantity demanded, then

PED would be $\dfrac{+15}{-15} = -1.0$

Demand is said to be unit elastic because a change in price has led to the same percentage change in quantity demanded.

When demand is unit elastic, the value of PED will be equal to 1 and the demand curve will be a rectangular hyperbola (see Figure 3.2).

(4) Perfectly inelastic demand

Suppose a 10% increase in the price of salt led to no change in the quantity demanded, then

PED would be $\dfrac{0}{10} = 0.0$

Demand is said to be perfectly price inelastic because a change in price has had no effect on quantity demanded.

When demand is perfectly price inelastic, the value of PED will be 0 and the demand curve will be vertical (see Figure 3.2).

(5) Perfectly elastic demand

Suppose a small increase in the price of a product causes the quantity demanded to fall to zero, then demand is said to be perfectly elastic.

When demand is perfectly elastic, the value of PED will be infinity and the demand curve will be horizontal (see Figure 3.2).

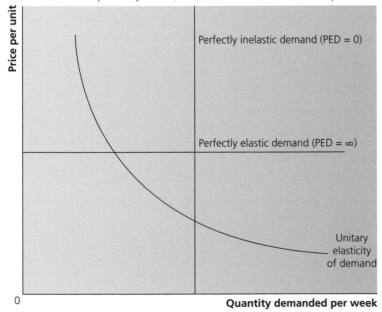

Figure 3.2 Demand curves showing unitary elasticity, perfectly inelastic and perfectly elastic demand

1 Calculate price elasticity of demand in the following examples and comment on your results:

(a) A rise in the price of electricity from 25 pence to 30 pence per unit causes the quantity demanded to fall from 10 000 kilos to 9000 kilos.

(b) A rise in the price of gold watches from $1000 to $1100 causes demand to fall from 200 to 170 per week.

(c) A 6% reduction in the price of tomatoes causes a 6% increase in quantity demanded.

Answer on p. 104

> **Examiner's tip**
>
> When considering whether demand is price elastic or price inelastic, compare the percentage changes in price and quantity. If the percentage change in quantity demanded is larger than the percentage price change, then demand is price elastic.

> **Examiner's tip**
>
> Think of perfectly inelastic demand as a set amount demanded whatever the price. The demand curve must therefore be vertical.

Price elasticity of demand and total revenue   Revised

There are key relationships between price elasticity of demand and **total revenue** (TR).

- When **demand is inelastic**, a price change causes total revenue to change in the **same direction**.
- When **demand is elastic**, a price change causes total revenue to change in the **opposite direction**.
- When **demand is unit elastic**, a price change causes total revenue to remain unchanged.
- When **demand is perfectly inelastic**, a price change causes total revenue to change in the **same direction by the same proportion**.
- When **demand is perfectly elastic**, a price rise causes total revenue to **fall to zero**.

> **Total revenue** is the value of goods sold by a firm and is calculated by multiplying price times quantity sold.

> **Typical mistake**
>
> To conclude that if a price change has no effect on total revenue, the demand is perfectly inelastic. This is incorrect: for total revenue to remain constant following a price change there must have been an exactly proportionate change in quantity demanded. In other words, demand is unit elastic.

Revision activity

The PED varies along a straight-line demand curve. You can check this yourself by completing the following table:

Price per unit (£)	Quantity demanded per week (kilos)	Total revenue	PED
10	10		
9	20		
8	30		
7	40		
6	50		
5	60		
4	70		
3	80		
2	90		
1	100		

Now test yourself · Tested

2 If the demand for petrol is price inelastic, what will happen to the total revenue of a garage selling petrol following an increase in price?

3 If a rise in the price of gold jewellery leads to a fall in the total revenue of shops selling this type of jewellery, what can be deduced about price elasticity of demand?

4 An increase in the price of iPads has no effect on total revenue. What can be inferred about the price elasticity of demand?

Answers on p. 104

Influencing factors · Revised

Factors which influence the price elasticity of demand include:

- **Availability of substitutes** — if substitutes are available there will be a strong incentive to shift consumption to these when the price of the product rises. The existence of substitutes will therefore tend to make demand for the product elastic.

- **Proportion of income spent on a product** — if only a small percentage of income is spent on a product such as salt then demand will tend to be inelastic, whereas if a high percentage of income is spent on the product then demand will tend to be elastic (e.g. exotic holidays; works of art by famous artists).

- **Nature of the product** — if the product is addictive (e.g. alcohol, tobacco) then demand will tend to be inelastic.

- **Durability of the product** — if the product is long lasting and hard wearing (e.g. furniture and cars) then demand will be fairly elastic since it is possible to postpone purchases. However, demand for non-durable goods (e.g. milk, petrol) will tend to be inelastic because these must be replaced regularly.

- **Length of time under consideration** — it usually takes time for consumers to adjust their expenditure patterns following a price change. For example, it will take time for motorists to switch from fuel-greedy cars to more fuel-efficient cars. Consequently demand is usually more price elastic in the long run than in the short run.

- **Breadth of definition of a product** — if a product is broadly defined (e.g. fruit), demand is likely to be price inelastic. However, demand for a particular type of fruit (e.g. apples) is likely to be more price elastic.

Typical mistake

Describing a product as elastic or inelastic: this is imprecise because this could relate to demand or supply. In the case of PED, it should be stated that *demand* for product X is elastic/inelastic.

Examiner's tip

It is not helpful to use the idea of luxuries and necessities as a factor influencing price elasticity of demand because what is a necessity or a luxury changes over time. This distinction is far too imprecise to have any value.

Now test yourself · Tested

5 Why is demand for a particular brand of rice likely to be price elastic?

6 Would you expect demand for coffee to be price elastic or inelastic?

7 Why might demand for milk be price inelastic?

Answers on p. 104

Significance for firms

Revised

If firms know that demand for their product is price inelastic then they know that they can increase total revenue by increasing price.

However, if firms know that demand is price elastic they can increase total revenue by reducing price. For example, if there are many restaurants in a high street then one of these might have special offers on certain days, knowing that this will increase their revenue.

Significance for the government

Revised

If the government wishes to maximise its tax revenue then it will place indirect taxes on those products whose demand is price inelastic (e.g. goods such as alcohol, petrol and tobacco). However, in this case the consumer will bear most of the tax burden.

The government may therefore also tax products and services whose demand is price elastic, in which case the producers will bear a higher proportion of the tax burden.

Cross elasticity of demand (XED)

Cross elasticity of demand is a measure of the responsiveness of the quantity demanded of one product (Y) to a change in the price of another product (X).

> **Cross elasticity of demand** is the sensitivity of demand for one product to a change in the price of another product.

Measuring cross elasticity of demand

Revised

$$XED = \frac{\text{percentage change in quantity demanded of Product Y}}{\text{percentage change in price of Product X}}$$

Interpreting results

Again for XED, **the sign** is very significant.

- A **positive sign** indicates that the products are **substitutes** (e.g. a rise in the price of one product will cause an increase in demand for another product).

- A **negative sign** indicates that the products are **complements** (e.g. a rise in the price of one product will cause a decrease in demand for another product).

> **Typical mistake**
>
> Misinterpreting the result of a calculation of XED. The key point is that if the result is positive, then the goods are substitutes and if negative then the goods are complements.

Now test yourself

Tested

8 For each of the following calculate the cross elasticity of demand and comment on your answer:

   (a) A 10% increase in the price of tea causes a 15% rise in the demand for coffee.

   (b) A 5% increase in the price of product Y causes a 10% decrease in the demand for product X.

Answers on p. 104

> **Examiner's tip**
>
> If the cross elasticity of demand is close to zero then it implies that the products are not closely related.

Value to businesses

A knowledge of cross elasticity of demand is helpful to businesses in setting prices for their products. For example, if a firm is selling a product with a close substitute then it would expect that demand for its product would fall considerably if it decided to increase its price.

Firms also know that complementary goods can command high prices. For example, printers are often relatively cheap but the ink cartridges required for them are relatively expensive because a certain type is required for each particular printer.

Income elasticity of demand (YED)

Income elasticity of demand is a measure of the responsiveness of the quantity demanded of a product to a change in real income.

Measuring income elasticity of demand

$$YED = \frac{\text{percentage change in quantity demanded}}{\text{percentage change in real income}}$$

Interpreting results

For YED, **the sign** is very significant. A **positive sign** indicates that the product is a **normal good**, i.e. a rise (fall) in real income will cause an increase (decrease) in demand. In contrast, a negative sign indicates that the product is an inferior good. Therefore, a rise in real income would cause a fall in demand.

> **Income elasticity of demand** is the sensitivity of demand for a product to a change in real income. (NB Real income discounts the effects of inflation.)

Examples

(1) Income elastic demand

If a 5% increase in real income leads to a 25% increase in demand then

$$YED = \frac{25}{5} = +5$$

Demand is income elastic because the change in real income has led to a more than proportionate change in demand. Whenever YED is greater than +1, demand is income elastic.

(2) Income inelastic demand

If a 10% increase in income causes a 3% increase in demand then

$$YED = \frac{3}{10} = +0.3$$

Demand is income inelastic because the change in real income has led to a less than proportionate change in demand. Whenever YED is between 0 and +1, demand is income inelastic.

(3) Inferior goods

A **negative sign** indicates that the product is an **inferior good** (e.g. a rise in real income leads to a fall in demand for the product).

If a 6% increase in real income resulted in a 3% fall in demand then YED would be negative:

$$YED = \frac{-3}{6} = -0.5$$

Inferior goods (as the name suggests) are those for which consumption will decline as real incomes increase because consumers can now afford higher-quality alternatives.

Typical mistake

Misinterpreting the result of a calculation of YED. The key point is that if the result is positive, then it is a normal good but if the result is negative then the good is an inferior good.

Examiner's tip

Inferior goods (those with a negative YED) are usually low-quality goods with more expensive substitutes.

The relationship between demand and income may be illustrated diagrammatically. For a normal good there is a positive relationship between income and demand but for an inferior good the relationship is negative, as shown in Figures 3.3a and 3.3b.

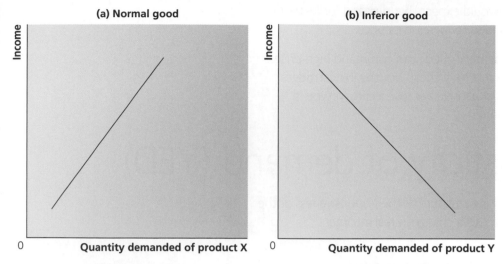

Figure 3.3 The relationship between demand and income

Now test yourself   Tested ☐

9   For each of the following calculate the income elasticity of demand
    and comment on your answer:
    (a) A 3% decrease in real incomes causes a 9% fall in the demand for
    new cars.
    (b) A 5% increase in real incomes causes a 2% fall in demand for
    soya.
    (c) A 10% increase in real incomes causes a 2% increase in the
    demand for oranges.

Answer on p. 104

Price elasticity of supply (PES)

Price elasticity of supply is a measure of the responsiveness of the quantity supplied of a product to a change in its price.

Measuring price elasticity of supply ——————————— Revised ☐

$$PES = \frac{\text{percentage change in quantity supplied}}{\text{percentage change in price}}$$

Price elasticity of supply is the sensitivity of supply of a product to a change in its price.

Interpreting results

PES will always have a positive value because price and quantity move in the same direction (since the supply curve is upward sloping).

(1) Price inelastic supply

Suppose a 10% increase in the price of wheat led to a 5% increase in quantity supplied, then

PES would be $\dfrac{5}{10}$ = 0.5

Supply is said to be price inelastic because a change in price has led to a smaller percentage change in quantity supplied. When supply is price inelastic, the value of PES will be between 0 and 1 (see Figure 3.4).

(2) Price elastic supply

Suppose a 2% decrease in the price of a laptop led to a 12% decrease in quantity supplied, then

PES would be $\dfrac{12}{2}$ = 6.0.

Supply is said to be price elastic because a change in price has led to a larger percentage change in quantity supplied. When supply is price elastic, the value of PES will be greater than 1 (see Figure 3.4).

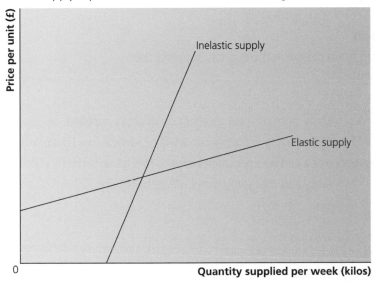

Figure 3.4 Inelastic and elastic supply

(3) Unit elasticity of supply

Suppose a 7% increase in the price of bread led to a 7% increase in quantity supplied, then

PES would be $\dfrac{7}{7}$ = 1.0.

Supply is said to be unit elastic because a change in price has led to the same percentage change in quantity supplied.

When supply is unit elastic, the value of PES will be equal to 1 and the supply curve will be a straight line drawn through the origin, as shown in Figure 3.5.

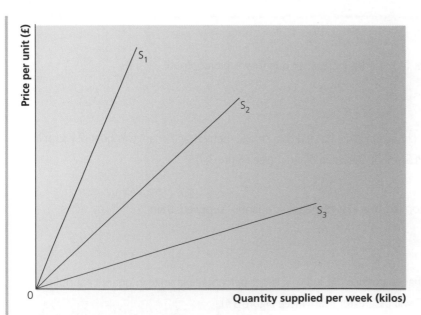

Figure 3.5 Unitary elasticity of supply

(4) Perfectly inelastic and perfectly elastic supply

Suppose a 10% increase in the price of a product led to no change in the quantity supplied, then

$$\text{PES would be } \frac{0}{10} = 0.0$$

Supply is said to be perfectly price inelastic because a change in price has had no effect on quantity supplied. When supply is perfectly price inelastic, the value of PES will be 0 and the supply curve will be vertical (see Figure 3.6). On the other hand, if an infinite amount could be supplied at a certain price, then supply is said to be perfectly elastic. When supply is perfectly elastic, the value of PES will be infinity and the supply curve will be horizontal.

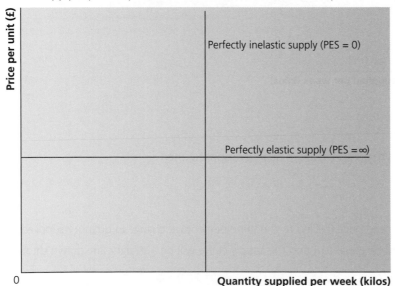

Figure 3.6 Elasticity of supply

10 For each of the following calculate the elasticity of supply and comment on your answer:

(a) A 20% increase in the price of lemons leads to a 2% increase in quantity supplied.

(b) A 5% fall in the price leads to a 15% reduction in the quantity supplied.

Answer on p. 104

> **Examiner's tip**
>
> A simple rule that applies to all elasticity calculations is that quantity is always at the top of the calculation.

Influencing factors   Revised ☐

Factors which influence the price elasticity of supply include:

- **Time** — it is often difficult to change supply quickly in response to a price change, making supply very inelastic in the short run. Therefore, the longer the time period under consideration, the more elastic supply is likely to be.

- **Stocks** — if stocks of finished goods are available, the supply will be relatively elastic because manufacturers will be able to respond quickly to a price change.

- **Spare capacity** — if a firm has under-utilised machinery and under-employed workers or if it is possible to introduce a new shift or workers, then supply is likely to be elastic.

- **Availability and cost of switching resources from use to another** — if resources (e.g. labour) have very specific skills, or machinery is highly specific, or it is expensive to reallocate resources from one use to another, then supply will be relatively inelastic.

11 Why might you expect the supply of tomatoes to be inelastic?

12 Under what circumstances might the supply of butter be elastic?

Answers on p. 104

> **Typical mistake**
>
> To consider factors influencing price elasticity of *demand* when asked to discuss the factors influencing the elasticity of *supply*. To avoid this error, remember that the factors influencing elasticity of supply are those affecting businesses, not consumers.

Consumers' surplus and producers' surplus

Consumers' surplus   Revised ☐

This refers to the difference between how much a person is willing to pay and how much they actually pay, i.e. the market price.

Diagrammatically, the **consumers' surplus** is the area under the demand curve and above the market price.

Factors affecting the size of consumers' surplus

- The gradient of the demand curve. The steeper it is, the greater will be the consumers' surplus.

- Changes in the conditions of demand. For example, an increase in demand will increase the amount of consumers' surplus.

> **Consumers' surplus** is the difference between how much consumers are willing to pay and what they actually pay for a product.

Producers' surplus

This refers to the difference between how much firms are willing to supply at each price and the market price.

Diagrammatically, the **producers' surplus** is the area between the supply curve and the market price.

> **Producers' surplus** is the difference between the cost of supply and the price received by the producer for the product.

Figure 3.7 illustrates both consumers' surplus and producers' surplus.

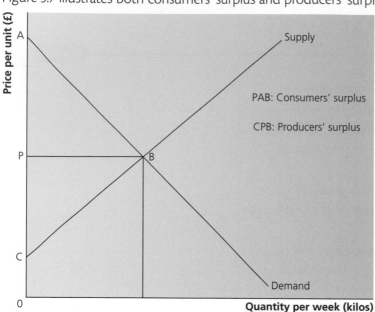

Figure 3.7 Consumers' and producers' surplus

Factors affecting the size of producers' surplus

- The gradient of the supply curve. The steeper it is, the greater will be the producers' surplus.

- Changes in the conditions of supply. For example, an increase in supply will increase the amount of producers' surplus.

> **Typical mistake**
>
> Confusing consumers' surplus with producers' surplus on a diagram. A simple way of avoiding this is to remember that producers' surplus relates to suppliers and so is the area above the supply curve and below the equilibrium price.

Exam practice

1 Total expenditure on Product X falls as price falls, but increases if income falls. What can be concluded from this information? [1+3]

	Price elasticity of demand	Income elasticity of demand
A	elastic	negative
B	elastic	positive
C	inelastic	positive
D	inelastic	negative

2 Product Y has a low price elasticity of supply. Which of the following could account for this?

A There are no close substitutes for Product Y.

B Product Y is addictive.

C Product Y is a heavily advertised brand of coffee.

D The specialist machinery required for Product Y is fully utilised. [1+3]

3 If a 7% increase in the price of Good X causes a 7% increase in the demand for Good Y then:

   A Goods X and Y are complements.

   B The price elasticity of demand for Good X is 1.

   C Goods X and Y are substitutes.

   D Cross elasticity of demand is −1.   [1+3]

4 100 000 jars of jam are demanded per day at £2 a jar. If the price elasticity of demand for these jars is −3 and the price is raised by 10%, the number of jars demanded per day would fall to:

   A 60 000

   B 70 000

   C 80 000

   D 90 000   [1+3]

5 An increase in demand for a product would cause:

   A Producers' surplus to increase.

   B Total revenue to fall.

   C Price to decrease.

   D Cross elasticity of demand to increase.   [1+3]

6 *Copper is used in wiring in a variety of electrical products and for making pipes; it has few good substitutes. In the decade since 2002, the price of copper has fluctuated between $1400 per tonne and $10 000 per tonne although the average price is much higher than at the beginning of the period. The fluctuations are closely linked to the state of the world economy: for example, in periods of high economic growth, demand for copper rises significantly. Higher average prices of copper have encouraged producers to open new mines but this takes a considerable time in finding new sources of supplies, gaining planning permission and building the mine.*

   (a) Would you expect demand for copper to be price elastic or price inelastic? Explain your answer.   [6]

   (b) What may be inferred about the income elasticity of demand for copper?   [6]

   (c) Assess the factors affecting the elasticity of supply of copper.   [8]

Answers and quick quizzes online

Online

Examiner's summary

You should have an understanding of:

✔ Price elasticity of demand: how it is calculated and how to interpret the results.

✔ The factors influencing price elasticity of demand.

✔ The relationship between price elasticity of demand and total revenue.

✔ Income elasticity of demand: how it is calculated and how to interpret the results.

✔ The distinction between normal goods and inferior goods.

✔ Cross elasticity of demand: how it is calculated and how to interpret the results.

✔ The distinction between complements and substitutes.

✔ Price elasticity of supply: how it is calculated and how to interpret the results.

✔ The factors influencing price elasticity of supply.

✔ Consumers' surplus and producers' surplus and the factors influencing each of these concepts.

4 Applications of supply and demand analysis

Indirect taxes and subsidies

Indirect taxes

Revised

Indirect taxes are taxes on expenditure and include taxes such as Value Added Tax (VAT), excise taxes and taxes on gambling. Such taxes cause an increase in the cost of supply and so cause the supply curve to shift to the left.

There are two types of **indirect taxes**: *ad valorem* and specific.

Ad valorem taxes

Ad valorem taxes are a percentage of the price of a product or service and so will cause the supply curve to shift to the left and become steeper than the original supply curve. An example of an *ad valorem* tax is VAT, currently levied at 20% in the UK.

> **Indirect taxes** are taxes on expenditure.
>
> **Ad valorem taxes** are a percentage of the price of the product.

Now test yourself

Tested

1 In 2011, VAT was increased from 17.5% to 20% in the UK. How would this have affected the supply curve for restaurant meals?

Answer on p. 104

Specific taxes

In contrast, a **specific tax**, or flat rate tax, is a set amount of tax on each unit consumed. Therefore the effect of a specific tax is to cause the supply curve to shift to the left, parallel to the original supply curve.

Figure 4.1 illustrates the impact of a specific tax when demand is inelastic.

> **Specific taxes** are a set amount per unit of the product.

> **Typical mistake**
>
> Wrongly assuming that an indirect tax causes the demand curve to shift to the left.

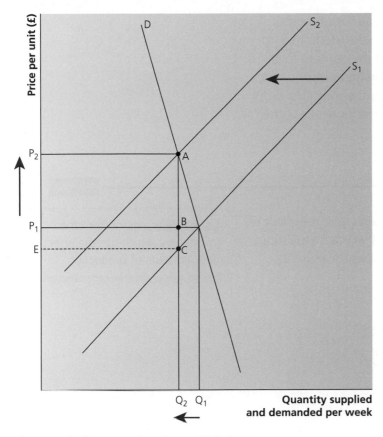

Figure 4.1 Indirect tax when demand is inelastic

P_1 is the initial equilibrium price and Q_1 is the initial equilibrium output. An indirect tax will cause the supply curve to shift to the left, from S_1 to S_2. In turn, this causes the price to increase to P_2 and the quantity to fall to Q_2. It can be seen that when demand is inelastic the consumer bears a much larger proportion of the tax burden (P_1P_2AB) whereas the producer bears a much smaller part of the tax burden (EP_1BC). This distribution of the tax burden is called the **incidence of tax**.

> **Incidence of tax** relates to how the burden of tax is distributed between different groups, e.g. consumers and producers

In contrast, Figure 4.2 illustrates the impact of a specific tax when demand is elastic.

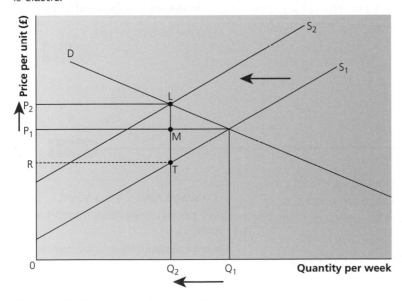

Figure 4.2 Indirect tax when demand is elastic

P_1 is the initial equilibrium price and Q_1 is the initial equilibrium output. An indirect tax will cause the supply curve to shift to the left, from S_1 to S_2. In turn, this causes the price to increase to P_2 and the quantity to fall to Q_2. It can be seen that when demand is elastic the producer bears a much larger proportion of the tax burden (RP_1MT) whereas the consumer bears a much smaller part of the tax burden (P_1P_2LM), i.e. the incidence of the tax falls mainly on producers.

Subsidies

A **subsidy** is a grant from the government. These grants have the effect of reducing costs of production. Consequently, subsidies will cause the supply curve to shift to the right. Figure 4.3 illustrates the impact of a subsidy.

> A **subsidy** is a grant from the government which has the effect of reducing costs of production.

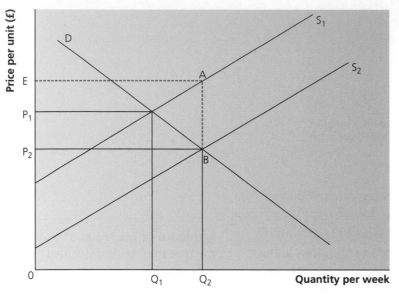

Figure 4.3 The effect of a subsidy

> **Typical mistake**
>
> Shifting the demand curve to the right to illustrate the effect of a subsidy. A subsidy affects suppliers and so affects the *supply* curve, not the demand curve.

The initial equilibrium price and quantity are P_1 and Q_1 but after the subsidy is granted by the government to producers the new equilibrium price falls to P_2 and the quantity rises to Q_2. AB represents the subsidy per unit and the total cost of the subsidy to the government is P_2EAB — i.e. the subsidy per unit multiplied by the quantity.

> **Now test yourself**
>
> 2 Explain the effect of a decrease in the subsidy for wind firms.
>
> Answers on p. 104
>
> Tested

The labour market

Wage determination

There are many markets for labour related to different occupations and industries. In a competitive market, the **wage rate** for a particular occupation or industry is determined by the forces of supply and demand. In practice, some labour markets are not competitive because, for example, the government may be the sole employer or a powerful trade union may control the supply of labour.

> The **wage rate** is the amount paid per hour/day/week/month for working.

The demand for labour

Revised

The demand for labour is a **derived demand**. This means that the demand for workers depends on the demand for the goods and services produced by those workers. For example, the rising demand for Jaguar Land Rover vehicles meant that a new shift of workers was employed in 2012.

The demand curve for labour shows the relationship between the real wage rate and the quantity of workers demanded. Typically, the demand curve for labour will be downward sloping because, as the real wage rate decreases, it becomes more attractive for firms to employ workers.

Influencing factors

Factors which influence the **elasticity of demand for labour** to a particular occupation or industry include:

- The elasticity of demand for the final product.
- The proportion of total costs accounted for by wage costs: if wage costs are a very high proportion of total cost then demand for labour will tend to be elastic.
- The ease/difficulty of replacing labour with machinery: if labour cannot easily be replaced with machinery then demand for labour will tend to be inelastic.

Factors which influence the **demand for labour** to a particular occupation or industry include:

- The demand for the final product.
- The relative price of capital and other factors: if labour costs rise relative to the cost of machinery, then firms are likely to replace labour with capital. For example, the cost of employing workers might be affected by changes in employers' national insurance contributions.
- The productivity of labour: a decrease in labour productivity (output per worker per hour worked) would cause a reduction in the demand for labour.
- The price of the product: a higher price would encourage firms to increase their demand for labour.
- Labour market regulations: if employment protection laws are increased, making it more difficult to hire and fire workers, then demand for labour is likely to fall.

If any of these factors change then the whole demand curve will shift.

> **Derived demand** is demand which is dependent on the demand for the final product.

> **Examiner's tip**
>
> The market for labour is analysed in a similar way to other competitive markets except that the demand for labour depends critically on the demand for the final product.

The supply of labour

Revised

The overall supply of labour depends on the size of the working population — i.e. all those over the school-leaving age who are willing and able to work.

The supply curve of labour for a particular industry or occupation shows how many people are willing to work at given wage rates. The supply curve will be upward sloping because, as real wages rise, there is more incentive for workers to transfer from other industries or for the unemployed to accept jobs or for those who are currently inactive to seek employment.

Figure 4.4 shows the equilibrium wage rate.

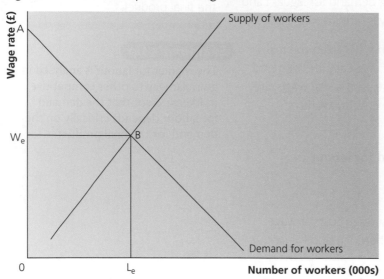

Figure 4.4 Equilibrium wage rate

Examiner's tip

In Unit 1, the emphasis is on the market for labour in a particular occupation.

Influencing factors

Factors which influence the **elasticity of supply of labour** to a particular occupation or industry include:

- Skills, qualifications and experience required: if these are high then the supply of labour will tend to be inelastic.
- Level of unemployment in the economy: if unemployment is high then supply is likely to be more elastic.

Changes in any of the following factors could cause a shift in the supply curve for labour in a particular occupation or industry.

- **Net migration:** a rise in immigration relative to emigration would cause a rightward shift in the supply curve.
- **The real wage in other occupations.** For example, a rise in real wages of engineers relative to other occupations would result in an increase in the supply of workers into the engineering industry.
- **Non-monetary factors** such as job satisfaction; job security; prospects of promotion; hours of work and holidays; private health care insurance; and pension rights.
- **Income tax rates.** For example, a reduction in income tax rates might encourage more people who are currently inactive to seek employment.
- **Qualifications and legal requirements:** if there is a new requirement for all entrants into an industry to be graduates then this is likely to decrease the supply of labour.
- **Childcare facilities and cost:** an improvement in childcare facilities at a lower cost is likely to result in an increased supply of labour, especially women.

Typical mistake

Confusing the factors influencing the demand for labour with those influencing the supply of labour. To avoid this remember that demand for labour is determined by the demand for the product whereas the supply of labour is dependent on the number of people willing to offer themselves for employment.

Now test yourself

Tested

3 What will be the effect on the wage rate of engineers of each of the following?
   (a) Net emigration of engineering graduates from the UK.
   (b) Increased expenditure on research into engineering products.
   (c) Increased sponsorship for vocational and university engineering courses.

Answer on p. 104

A National Minimum Wage

Many governments have introduced a **National Minimum Wage** (NMW). This is a legally binding wage which prevents employers paying an hourly wage less than a set amount.

> The **National Minimum Wage** is a rate set by the government to specify the lowest legal amount that workers can be paid.

Aim of the NMW

Revised

The main aim of the NMW is to prevent the exploitation of workers and to reduce inequality.

Figure 4.5 illustrates the effect of the government setting a NMW above the free market level.

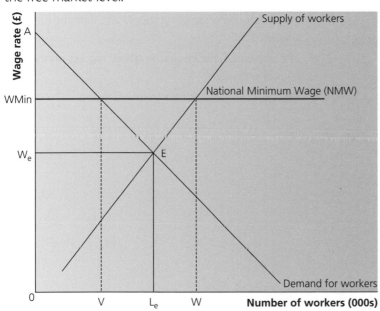

Figure 4.5 The effect of a National Minimum Wage

Figure 4.5 shows the equilibrium wage is W_e and the equilibrium quantity of workers is L_e. If the National Minimum Wage is set at WMin then the amount of labour demanded is 0V but the amount supplied will be 0W. Consequently, there is surplus labour, i.e. unemployment of VW.

The amount of unemployment in this industry will be determined by the following factors.

● How high the NMW is relative to the equilibrium wage.
● The price elasticity of demand for labour.
● The price elasticity of supply of labour.

> **Examiner's tip**
>
> The analysis of the National Minimum Wage is simply an application of excess supply, as described above under the topics of the demand for/supply of labour.

Now test yourself

4 What is the likely effect of an increase in the National Minimum Wage on the restaurant business and the wages of waiters?

Answer on p. 104

Tested

Exam practice

1 A decrease in the National Minimum Wage for agricultural workers is likely to:

   A Increase the shortage of agricultural workers.

   B Increase unemployment amongst agricultural workers.

   C Cause a contraction in the supply of agricultural workers.

   D Cause an extension of demand for agricultural workers.   **[1+3]**

2 Producers of green energy receive a subsidy from the government. This will cause:

   A A leftward shift in the supply curve for green energy.

   B A decrease in consumers' surplus.

   C A fall in the price of green energy.

   D A decrease in the number of firms providing green energy.   **[1+3]**

3 *In 2011, the rate of VAT was increased from 17.5% to 20% on most goods and services. The effect on prices and output has varied depending on the price elasticity of demand for different goods and services.*

   (a) Assuming demand is price elastic, explain and illustrate the effect of an increase in VAT on laptops.   **[6]**

   (b) In the above example, will producers or consumers bear most of the tax burden?   **[4]**

Answers and quick quizzes online

Online

Examiner's summary

You should have an understanding of:

✔ The effect of indirect taxes and subsidies using supply and demand analysis.

✔ Factors influencing the demand for labour and the supply of labour.

✔ Wage determination using supply and demand analysis.

✔ The impact of changes in the labour market on the equilibrium wage.

✔ The effects of a National Minimum Wage.

5 Market failure

The term **market failure** is used to describe the failure of the market system to allocate resources efficiently. It arises because the price mechanism has not taken into account all the costs and/or benefits in the production or consumption of the product or service.

> **Market failure** occurs when the forces of supply and demand (market forces) do not result in the efficient allocation of resources.

Reasons for market failure

There are various reasons why the free market system may fail including:

- immobility of labour
- public goods
- externalities: negative externalities and positive externalities
- price instability in commodity markets
- asymmetric information
- government failure

Examiner's tip

Ensure that you know that there are several forms of market failure. The list given here is not complete. For example, other forms of market failure include monopoly and inequality; these are not required for this unit but do form part of the A2 specification.

For resources to be allocated efficiently, it is necessary for social marginal costs (SMC) to be equal to social marginal benefits (SMB). In practice, some costs and/or benefits may not be included because they may not be known or may be difficult to quantify. Social marginal cost refers to the addition to total cost of producing an extra unit of output, whereas social marginal benefit refers to the addition to total benefits of consuming an extra unit.

Now test yourself Tested ☐

1 How can a market fail?
2 What condition must be met for resources to be allocated efficiently?

Answers on p. 104

Immobility of labour

This refers to barriers or limitations on the ability of workers to move between different parts of the country or between occupations.

Two types of labour immobility are usually distinguished:

- **geographical immobility of labour**
- **occupational immobility of labour**

> **Geographical immobility of labour** involves factors which limit the movement of workers from one region of the country to another.
>
> **Occupational immobility of labour** involves factors which limit the movement of workers from one occupation to another.

Geographical immobility of labour Revised ☐

This refers to limitations or restrictions on the ability of workers to move from one part of the country to another.

Causes

The causes of geographical immobility of labour include:

- Differences in regional house prices: this is often regarded as the most significant barrier to the mobility of labour because a person living in an area of relatively low house prices will find it very difficult to move to an area where house prices are much higher.
- Costs of moving house: these include removal costs; legal costs; and taxes. Such costs may be considerable and, therefore, act as a real barrier to geographical mobility.
- Social and family ties: some people may be reluctant to move away from an area because they have family and friends in the area and/or have other links to the area.
- Disruption of children's education: parents may be unwilling to move to a different part of the country as it means that their children must change schools.

Measures to increase the geographical mobility of labour

Governments may use a variety of policies to increase the mobility of labour including:

- Housing subsidies: these could take the form of rent subsidies or housing benefit.
- The provision of affordable housing: the government may build new homes for those on low incomes or provide a scheme where the buyer has a part-share in the ownership of the house.
- Reduction in planning restrictions so that it is easier for developers to build new houses.
- Improvement of information about job availability in other parts of the country (e.g. through the internet).

Examiner's tip

Be prepared to illustrate the effect of rent subsidies using a supply and demand diagram.

Now test yourself

Tested

3 Which of the following would help to increase the geographical mobility of labour?
(a) A decrease in house prices in areas of high unemployment.
(b) An increase in removal costs.
(c) A decrease in the stamp duty payable on buying a new house.
(d) An increase in the number of training schemes provided by the government.
(e) Provision of new, cheap rented accommodation in all parts of the country.

Answer on p. 104

Occupational immobility of labour

Revised

This refers to limitations or restrictions on the ability of workers to move from one occupation to another.

Causes

The causes of occupational immobility of labour include:

- Lack of relevant skills: unemployed workers may be unable to secure jobs because they do not have the skills required to take the jobs available.

Typical mistake

Confusing geographical and occupational mobility of labour. To avoid this remember that geography relates to places, so geographical immobility refers to the difficulties of moving from one part of the country to another.

- Lack of appropriate qualifications: for some jobs a specific qualification may be required.
- No relevant experience: some employers insist on the need for experience in the occupation before employing a worker.
- Wage rate: a worker may not wish to move to another job if the wage rate is too low.

Measures to increase the occupational mobility of labour

These include:

- Training programmes: these would be aimed at closing skills shortages by providing appropriate courses.
- Increase higher education provision: graduates may have transferable skills so that they can be trained quickly and easily to work in different occupations.
- Information about opportunities in other occupations: workers may not be aware of the possibility of pursuing an alternative career.

> **Examiner's tip**
>
> To determine which measure is appropriate for each type of immobility, ask yourself whether it would help to increase movement from one part of the country to another (geographical mobility) or from one job to another (occupational mobility).

> **Now test yourself**   Tested ☐
>
> 4 Which of the following would cause an increase in the occupational immobility of labour?
>   (a) An improvement in the number of vocational courses available free of change.
>   (b) Housing subsidies.
>   (c) An increase in the qualifications required for certain jobs.
>   (d) A new website providing information available about job opportunities in different industries.
>
> Answer on p. 104

Public goods

The characteristic which makes **public goods** unique is that the benefits they provide affect many people rather than just one individual. This is in contrast to private goods which are rival and excludable — i.e. consumption of a good by one person means that it cannot be consumed by anyone else and that it is not available to anyone else.

> **Public goods** are those goods which have two key characteristics — i.e. they are non-rivalrous (amount available does not fall after one person's consumption) and non-excludable (cannot prevent anyone from consuming them).

Characteristics of public goods ———————————— Revised ☐

Pure public goods have two special characteristics which distinguish them from private goods.

- **Non-rivalrous**: this means that consumption by one person does not limit consumption by others — i.e. the benefit to others is not reduced by one person's consumption.
- **Non-excludability**: this means that if a good is available for one person, then it is available for everyone — i.e. it is impossible to prevent or exclude anyone from using it.

> **Now test yourself**
>
> 5 How do private goods differ from public goods?
>
> Answer on p. 104
>
> Tested ☐

The free rider problem

Revised

These characteristics mean that when a public good is provided by someone, other people will be able to benefit from it without paying — in other words, they get a '**free ride**'. This is a problem because in such circumstances the market will fail: an insufficient number of people will be willing to pay for the product and it will not be profitable for a business to provide it.

> **Free rider problem** — the problem that once a product is provided it is impossible to prevent people from using it and, therefore, impossible to charge for it.

Typical mistake

Assuming that all goods provided by the state, such as health and education, are public goods. This is not necessarily true because health and education are also provided by the private sector.

Now test yourself

6 Why does the free rider problem occur?

Answer on p. 104

Tested

Examples of public goods

Revised

It is arguable whether there are any examples of pure public goods displaying the characteristics of those described above but examples commonly used include:

● street lighting
● nuclear defence systems
● national parks

Now test yourself

7 How is technology used to charge consumers for television signals

Answer on p. 104

Tested

Policy to correct the market failure

Revised

The usual policy response is for the government to provide public goods financed through taxation. A disadvantage of this approach is that ultimately politicians will determine the amount of resources allocated to these public goods without direct reference to the electorate.

Alternative methods of providing some public goods could be by agencies appointed by the government (known as 'contracting-out') or by charities and voluntary organisations.

Externalities

These are costs and benefits to third parties who are not directly part of a transaction between producers and consumers. They are, in effect, spillover effects arising from the production or consumption of a product or service which are not taken into account by the price mechanism.

Externalities and market failure

Revised

Externalities are a form of market failure because market forces will not result in an efficient allocation of resources.

Two types of externality may be distinguished:
● negative externalities
● positive externalities

Examiner's tip

Think of externalities as effects on stakeholders (e.g. consumers; firms; workers; the government) who are not part of a transaction between others.

Negative externalities (external costs)

These are costs to third parties — i.e. other than to the producer or consumer directly involved in the transaction. They are spillover costs from the production or consumption which the market fails to take into account.

External costs of production   Revised ☐

External costs of production include:

- air pollution (e.g. noxious gases from a factory)
- noise pollution (e.g. from building work associated with a new factory or from machinery used in the production process)
- pollution arising from the destruction of the rain forest to grow crops

> **External costs** are the costs in excess of private costs which affect third parties who are not part of the transaction.

Private costs   Revised ☐

Private costs are those costs paid directly by the producer and consumer in a transaction.

- Private costs of a producer: typically these will include, wages, rent, raw materials, energy.
- Private costs for a consumer: the cost to the consumer is usually the price paid for the product/service.

> **Private costs** are the direct costs to producers and consumers for producing and consuming a product.

Analysis of external costs of production   Revised ☐

The following formulae help to explain the concept of external costs:

    social costs = private costs + external costs

Therefore

    external costs = social costs – private costs

> **Social costs** are the sum of private costs and external costs.

The external costs of production diagram

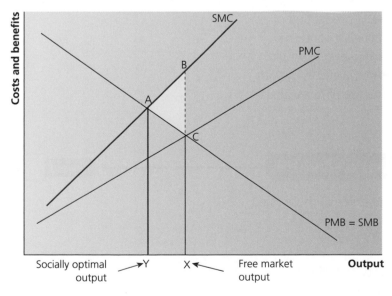

Figure 5.1 External costs of production

> **Typical mistake**
> Drawing a basic supply and demand curve when considering externalities.

- The private marginal benefit curve (PMB) shown in Figure 5.1 is the demand curve and indicates that private benefits to the consumer decrease as consumption increases. In this case, it is assumed that there are no external benefits so the PMB will be the same as the social marginal benefit (SMB) curve.

- The private marginal cost (PMC) curve is the supply curve and indicates that the private costs of providing the product rise as output rises.

- In a free market economy, therefore, the equilibrium will be determined from the equilibrium point at which PMB = PMC which will be output 0X.

- However, 0X would not be the socially optimal level of output because no account has been taken of the external costs of production.

- The social marginal cost (SMC) curve includes both the private costs and external costs and is, therefore, drawn to the left of the PMC curve.

- The socially optimal level of output is determined from the equilibrium point at which SMC = SMB which will be 0Y.

Welfare loss

- It can be seen that in a free market economy there is over-production and over-consumption of XY.

- This results in a welfare loss, shown as ABC in Figure 5.1.

> **Examiner's tip**
>
> External costs are an extra cost, so this means that the social marginal cost curve must be to the left of the private marginal cost.

> **Typical mistake**
>
> Welfare loss area identified incorrectly. To avoid this error, remember that at the free market output, the social marginal cost is greater than the social marginal benefit — use this information to determine the welfare loss.

External costs of consumption — Revised

These arise from consumption of products which have undesirable effects on third parties. For example, smoking might adversely affect the health of non-smokers, or waste from consumers might require more landfill sites which spoil the landscape.

External costs and sustainability — Revised

The issue of sustainability was referred to in Chapter 1. Environmental damage and the use of non-renewable resources in the production of goods and services might have implications for sustainability and this provides the rationale for government intervention. However, it should be noted that there have been significant increases in the efficiency with which resources are used as well as an increase in the use of renewable resources in production.

External costs: policies to correct market failure — Revised

Governments intervene in a variety of ways. The first three of those listed below operate through the market.

Indirect taxation

The aim of this strategy is to internalise the externality by taxing the product so that output and consumption will be at the level at which SMB = SMC. This is illustrated in Figure 5.2.

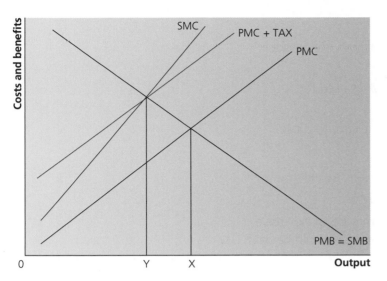

Figure 5.2 The taxing of a firm producing external costs

It can be seen that the tax will cause a leftward shift in the supply curve. If judged correctly, the tax will cause consumption and output to fall to 0Y, the socially optimum level.

Key advantages:

- incentive to reduce pollution
- source of revenue for the government and few costs administering this method

Key disadvantages:

- ineffective in reducing pollution if demand is price inelastic
- difficulty of setting an appropriate tax because of the problem of quantifying the external cost

Tradable permits

Tradable permits are issued to firms, up to a certain limit, by the government. Any pollution above the limit is subject to fines. The key to this system is that the permits may be traded between firms; firms which are 'clean' can sell their surplus permits to firms which are more polluting.

Key advantages:

- incentive for firms to reduce pollution
- the costs of administering such schemes are low relative to those associated with systems of regulation

Key disadvantages:

- pollution will continue, albeit at a lower level than previously
- large, efficient firms might buy up the permits and continue to pollute

Extension of property rights

This involves assigning ownership rights (**property rights**) to those who might be affected by external costs. Property rights therefore give the owners a right to claim damages against those causing the external cost. This is another method of bringing the private costs of an activity closer to its social costs.

Tradable permits, according to the OECD, are rights to sell and buy actual or potential pollution in artificially created markets.

Property rights are the exclusive authority to determine how a resource is used, whether that resource is owned by government, collective bodies, or individuals. In other words, property rights are really ownership rights.

Key advantages:

- there is an incentive for firms to take into account both the private costs and the external costs
- firms caught polluting could be fined and the money used to compensate those damaged
- the costs of administering these schemes are low relative to those associated with systems of regulation

Key disadvantages:

- there is the initial problem of assigning property rights
- if a breach of property rights has occurred, there may be an expensive legal procedure to determine how much compensation should be paid and to whom
- it may be difficult to agree on the monetary value of the external cost

Legal restrictions

Measures could include:

- a complete ban on the product
- regulations which place limits on the production process or on the amount of pollution allowed

In theory, this should restrict pollution to the required level, but without enforcement firms may not meet the legal requirements. To ensure that the law is upheld, considerable enforcement costs (e.g. inspectors) may be required.

Now test yourself　　　　　　　　　　　　　　　　　　　　　　　　`Tested`

8　A firm producing chemicals pays another firm for its raw materials and pays an average wage of £35 000 to its workers. It discharges its waste into a river adjacent to the factory which causes the fish to die. Fishermen downstream suffer from a loss of income. Farmers pay the chemical company £100 per kilo for the fertiliser produced by the chemical company.

　　(a) In the above extract, which are private costs and which are external costs?

　　(b) What factors make it difficult to determine how much tax to place on a company producing external costs?

Answer on p. 104

Positive externalities (external benefits)

These are benefits to third parties — i.e. other than to the producer or consumer directly involved in the transaction. They are spillover benefits from the production or consumption which the market fails to take into account.

External benefits of consumption　　　　　　　　　　　　　　`Revised`

External benefits of consumption include:

- commercially owned bees pollinating the fruit trees of local farmers
- households with well-kept gardens increasing the market value of neighbouring properties
- a chemical firm discharging clean water increasing the productivity of a trout farm downstream

> **External benefits** are benefits in excess of private benefits which affect third parties who are not part of the transaction.

Private benefits

Private benefits are those received directly by the producer and consumer in a transaction.

- Private benefits to a producer: typically these will include the revenues received from the sale of the product/service.
- Private benefits to a consumer: the utility (satisfaction) gained by the consumer from the consumption of the product/service.

> **Private benefits** are direct benefits to producers and consumers for producing and consuming a product.

Analysis of external benefits of consumption

The following formula helps to explain the concept of external benefits.

social benefits = private benefits + external benefits

Therefore

external benefits = social benefits − private benefits

> **Social benefits** are the sum of private benefits and external benefits.

The external benefits of consumption diagram

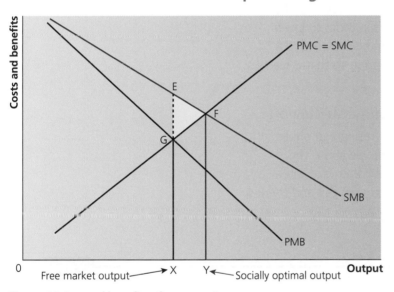

Figure 5.3 External benefits of consumption

> **Typical mistake**
>
> Welfare gain area identified incorrectly. To avoid this error, remember that at the free market output the social marginal benefit is greater than the social marginal cost — use this information to determine the welfare loss.

- The private marginal benefit curve (PMB) is the demand curve and indicates that private benefits to the consumer decrease as consumption increases.
- The private marginal cost (PMC) curve is the supply curve. In this case, it is assumed that there are no external costs so the PMC will be the same as the social marginal cost (SMC) curve.
- In a free market economy, therefore, the equilibrium will be determined from the equilibrium point at which PMB = PMC which will be output 0X.
- However, 0X would not be the socially optimal level of output because no account has been taken of the external benefits of production.
- The social marginal benefit (SMB) curve includes both the private benefits and external benefits and is, therefore, drawn to the right of the PMB curve.
- The socially optimal level of output is determined from the equilibrium point at which SMC = SMB which will be 0Y.

Potential welfare gain

- It can be see that in a free market economy there is under-production and under-consumption of XY.
- If the socially optimum output is produced, then there will be a welfare gain, shown as EFG in Figure 5.3.

External benefits: policies to correct market failure

Governments could use the following methods of increasing production and consumption to the socially optimal level.

Provision by the state

The government might decide that the most efficient way of dealing with this type of market failure is by state provision, funded by tax revenues. For example, the UK has a National Health Service (NHS) which provides many services free at the point of use.

Subsidies

The government might provide grants to producers in order to lower production costs so that the product or service can be provided at a lower price. In turn, this should encourage consumption so that it reaches the socially optimal level.

Measures to encourage changes in consumer behaviour

The most obvious example of this approach is advertising and public information films which are designed to educate people about the benefits of a certain course of action (e.g. to have children vaccinated against measles). Obviously there is a cost associated with this and there is no guarantee that the policy will be effective.

External benefits of production

These arise from the production of goods and services which benefit third parties. For example, a beekeeper keeps bees to produce honey but the bees also pollinate the fruit trees of local farmers.

Unstable commodity prices

Causes of commodity price instability

- The main source of price instability relates to the price inelasticity of supply and demand.
- Supply is inelastic because a long growing period is required for soft commodities (e.g. most agricultural commodities) while for hard commodities (e.g. coal, diamonds) considerable time is required for developing new mines.
- Demand is usually price inelastic for commodities because they are required in the production of other goods for which demand is also price inelastic (e.g. pasta, bread, steel).

- Consequently, any shift in the supply curve or demand curve would cause a sharp change in price. For example, the 2012 drought in the USA caused a reduction in the supply of corn, soya and sweetcorn. Given the inelasticity of demand, this resulted in large percentage increases in the prices of these commodities.

Examiner's tip

Although supply-side shocks are usually the cause of commodity price fluctuations, it is also possible that sudden changes in demand will cause significant price changes.

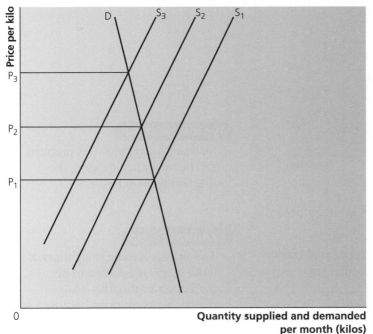

Figure 5.4 Price instability in commodity markets

Figure 5.4 illustrates that the drought in the USA caused a leftward shift in the supply curve for wheat. The demand for wheat is price inelastic because it is a staple product used in the production of many basic products such as bread. Consequently there is a significant increase in the price of wheat.

Similarly, a change in demand would cause a significant price change because supply is price inelastic. In the last decade, the prices of many commodities has increased because demand has increased. There are a number of reasons for this including:

- an increase in the world population (now over 7 billion)
- an increase in real incomes which has led to increased demand for many commodities (e.g. the demand for beef has increased significantly, which in turn raises the requirement for grain for animal feed)
- an increased demand for grain to be used for fuel

Now test yourself

9 Why do the prices of commodities tend to fluctuate more than the prices of manufactured goods?

Answer on p. 105

Tested ☐

Buffer stock schemes
Revised ☐

One method of reducing price instability is to adopt schemes which involve storing and releasing the commodity in times of surplus and shortage. The following analysis describes one way by which a **buffer stock scheme** might operate.

- A ceiling price: this is the maximum price which would be allowed.
- A floor price: this is the minimum price which would be allowed.
- A buffer stock would be established: this could be operated either by a government or by a producers' association. It would store or release stocks as required in order to reduce price fluctuations to the agreed limits.

A **buffer stock scheme** is designed to reduce price fluctuations which involves setting a ceiling and a floor price, and buying and selling stocks to maintain price within these limits.

Figure 5.5 illustrates the operation of a buffer stock scheme.

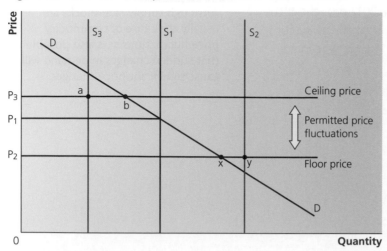

Figure 5.5 A buffer stock scheme

- In Year 1, the equilibrium price is P_1 so no action is required because the price is within the permitted price range.
- Suppose supply is S_2 is year 2 then, to prevent the price from falling below the floor price, xy would be removed from the market and stored in a buffer stock.
- If supply fell to S_3 in year 3, then to prevent the price rising above the ceiling level, ab would be released from the buffer stock.

Critique of buffer stock schemes

In practice, many problems are associated with these schemes.

- If the floor price is set too high, then there will be surpluses each year.
- Equally, if the ceiling price is set too low there may be insufficient stocks available in years of shortage.
- These schemes involve costs of storage.
- Success depends on ensuring that all the major producers agree to be part of the scheme and that none of them cheats (e.g. by selling to a major consumer at a reduced price).

Typical mistake

Inaccurate diagrams. This problem can be minimised by using the diagram given in Figure 5.5.

Examiner's tip

The analysis is more straightforward if the supply is assumed to be perfectly inelastic. This is a reasonable assumption because a set amount will be produced each year.

Now test yourself   Tested ☐

10 What is the main purpose of buffer stock schemes?
11 Under what circumstances is a buffer stock scheme most likely to be successful?

Answers on p. 105

Minimum guaranteed prices ────────────────────── Revised ☐

An alternative system would be for the government to set a minimum guaranteed price (MGP) for a particular commodity. This means that producers know in advance that they will receive a certain price per kilo no matter how much is produced.

A minimum guaranteed price is a price, usually set by the government, which is guaranteed to producers.

Figure 5.6 illustrates the effects of a minimum guaranteed price scheme.

Exam practice answers and quick quizzes at **www.hodderplus.co.uk/myrevisionnotes**

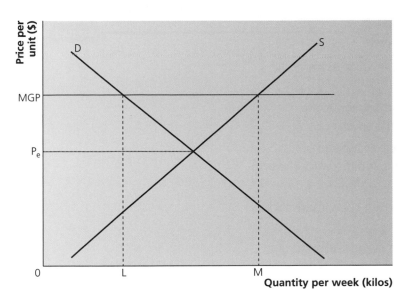

Figure 5.6 A minimum guaranteed price scheme

- The equilibrium price is P_e.
- Suppose the government sets a minimum guaranteed price (MGP) above the equilibrium price.
- This will result in a surplus of LM kilos.
- The government will buy this surplus and store it for years in which there is a shortage.

Advantages

The advantages of minimum guaranteed prices include:

- producers know in advance the price they will receive for their product
- this greater certainty enables producers to plan investment and output

Disadvantages

The problems associated with minimum guaranteed prices are similar to those of buffer stock schemes:

- if the minimum guaranteed price is set too high, then there will be surpluses each year
- these schemes involve costs of storage which must be borne by taxpayers
- these schemes encourage over-production and may, therefore, result in an inefficient allocation of resources

Asymmetric information

The free market system is based on the assumption that consumers and producers make rational choices and decisions based on perfect and equal market knowledge. In practice, this assumption may be unrealistic. For example, producers may have more information than consumers about a product or service, or consumers may simply not have sufficient information to make a rational decision. As a result of this **asymmetric information**, resources may be allocated inefficiently, resulting in market failure.

Asymmetric information is a situation in which one party in a transaction has more or superior information compared to another.

Examples of asymmetric information

The following provide some examples of markets in which asymmetric information is possible.

- **Housing market** — estate agents may know more about the potential problems of a house than the potential buyer.
- **Life insurance** — the consumer may not reveal all aspects of his health profile to the insurance company, making it difficult for the firm to assess risk.
- **Second-hand car sales** — the car salesperson will know more about the car than a potential buyer.
- **Financial services** — a bank may be unaware of the likelihood of a default by the borrower.
- **High-tech products** — consumers are unlikely to have as much information as producers about products such as smart phones and computer games.

Dealing with asymmetric information

Many of those methods used for dealing with the issue of public goods may be employed. For example:

- state provision (e.g. in the case of pensions)
- public information/advertisements designed to close the information gap
- private sector organisations, the media and the internet: information gaps may be closed by publications which inform consumers about issues concerning products and services

> **Examiner's tip**
>
> Remember that asymmetric information and incomplete information are a form of market failure because they restrict the ability of consumers and producers to make rational choices.

Government failure

Government failure arises as a result of government intervention in a market in an attempt to correct a market failure. This causes output and consumption to move further away from the socially efficient level. In other words, government failure is a situation in which government intervention would result in a more inefficient allocation of resources, leading to a net welfare loss.

> **Government failure** is when government intervention results in a net welfare loss.

> **Typical mistake**
>
> Confusing government failure with market failure.

Examples of government failure

Government intervention in a market may have unforeseen and undesirable consequences. The following are examples where government failure might be observed.

- **Agricultural stabilisation schemes** (e.g. buffer stock schemes and minimum guaranteed prices). As explained previously, these schemes could result in massive surpluses which would involve huge storage costs. Further, such surpluses imply that resources may not be allocated efficiently. For example, in the case of wheat, it might suggest that land should be used for alternative crops.

- **Housing policies** — state provision of housing at low rents might be considered desirable for those on low incomes. However, housing subsidies prevent the market from working efficiently (e.g. there is little incentive for people to move even if their incomes rise, so limiting the geographical mobility of labour).

- **Environmental policies** — subsidies have been given for the establishment of wind farms but many argue that the energy produced for them is relatively expensive and that they are themselves an environmental problem (eyesore).

- **The labour market** — many governments have introduced a National Minimum Wage for workers. However, it is argued that this could result in unemployment if the wage is set above the free market wage. The rate of unemployment will depend on how much the minimum wage is above the equilibrium wage and on the price elasticity of demand and price elasticity of supply of labour.

These are just a few examples but a case can be made for many other examples, including government intervention in the fishing industry (which may actually cause the depletion of fish stocks) and high taxes on alcohol and tobacco (which might encourage smuggling to such an extent that a further tax rise causes a fall in tax revenues).

Exam practice

1 Public goods:

   A are under-provided in a free market economy

   B are those used by consumers

   C are called 'free goods'

   D always cost less than private goods.   [1+3]

2 Car repair firms might undertake non-essential work on cars for their customers and charge them for this work because:

   A This will reduce the profits of car repair firms.

   B There are very few car repair firms.

   C There is asymmetric information.

   D Customers always consider external benefits when making decisions.   [1+3]

3 When a government increased the tax on whisky the tax revenue fell despite an increase in sales because there was increased tax evasion. This illustrates:

   A The high marginal social benefit of drinking whisky.

   B An example of an inferior good.

   C The low marginal private benefit of drinking whisky.

   D An example of government failure.   [1+3]

4 *It has been estimated that an economics graduate can earn significantly more than a student with 2 A-levels. Research suggests that graduates secure more interesting and satisfying jobs than non-graduates. A highly skilled workforce might attract more foreign direct investment. Further, graduates learn transferable skills which can help to increase productivity. Both these factors, therefore, help to increase economic growth of the country.*

   Tuition fees were increased from £3375 in 2011 to £9000 in 2012. This resulted in a 10% fall in applications to English universities. The government argues that the private benefits of going to university are significant so the increase in fees is justified. Free market economists suggest that government subsidies to universities encourage inefficiency and a lack of responsiveness to market demand. Further, many courses may offer no benefit to the economy.

(a) What might be the opportunity cost to the government of funding universities? [4]

(b) Explain the private costs for an individual student of a university education. [6]

(c) Assess the private and external benefits of university education. [14]

(d) Evaluate the economic arguments for an increase in university tuition fees. [14]

(e) From the information provided, calculate the price elasticity of demand for university education. Critically examine your result. [10]

5 *World food prices increased dramatically in 2007 and in the first half of 2008. After a rapid fall in prices in the latter part of 2008, they increased again from 2009 to 2011. Further price rises occurred in 2012.*

The causes of these price rises are wide-ranging: extreme weather conditions, such as droughts, have played a significant role while rising oil prices have been blamed for raising the costs of fertilisers, food transportation, and industrial agriculture.

Other fundamental causes include the increasing use of biofuels in developed countries and an increasing demand for a more varied diet across the expanding middle-class populations of Asia.

In some years stocks of agricultural commodities have prevented sharper price increases.

(a) Under what circumstances might the short-run supply curve for agricultural commodities be price elastic? [6]

(b) Assess the causes of food price rises, illustrating your answer with a supply and demand diagram. [14]

(c) Comment on the cross elasticity of demand between wheat and oil. [6]

(d) Assess the effect of rising food prices on the demand for other goods and services. [8]

(e) Evaluate buffer stock schemes as a means of reducing food price fluctuations. [14]

Answers and quick quizzes online

Online

Examiner's summary

You should have an understanding of:

✔ The meaning of market failure and the different forms of market failure.

✔ Immobility of labour: causes of geographical and occupational immobility and possible ways of increasing mobility of labour.

✔ Negative and positive externalities.

✔ Diagrams depicting external costs of production and external benefits of consumption.

✔ The reasons why commodity prices are unstable.

✔ Methods of reducing price instability: buffer stock schemes and minimum guaranteed prices.

✔ Public goods and their key characteristics: non-rivalry and non-excludability; the free rider problem.

✔ Methods of providing public goods.

✔ Asymmetric information: meaning and significance.

✔ Ways of dealing with asymmetric information.

✔ Government failure: meaning and causes.

6 Measuring economic performance

Economic growth

Measuring growth
Revised

Economic growth is a measure of an increase in **real** gross domestic product (GDP). GDP is the total amount of goods and services produced in a country in one year, or the total amount spent, or the total amount earned.

Potential economic growth is a measure of the increase in capacity in an economy. It can be shown by a movement outwards of the PPF curve (see Chapter 1 page 13). It is a measure of how efficient the economy is in using its resources.

If an economy has two consecutive quarters (three months, starting January, April, July or October) of negative economic growth then it is in a **recession**. The UK went into recession in 2008 and after a brief period of growth in 2010 to 2011 there was a return to recession in 2012. A recession means that there is less spending, income and output in the economy. It is likely to lead to firms closing, increased unemployment and a resulting fall in living standards.

> **Real** means that inflation has been taken into account. Real values are sometimes referred to as 'constant prices'. If inflation is left in the figures they are known as nominal or current.
>
> **Recession** — if an economy has two consecutive quarters (three months, starting January, April, July or October) of negative economic growth then it is in a recession. Sometimes a country comes out of recession and quickly goes back in again, as with the UK in 2012, a so-called double dip recession.

Now test yourself
Tested

1   What is a double dip recession?

Answer on p. 105

Changing living standards
Revised

An increase in GDP is likely to cause an increase in **standards of living**, which means that people can afford more goods and services, or feel that their lives are better because they do not need to work as hard to achieve their requirements in life.

However, a rising income does not necessarily make standards of living rise. It depends on how the extra money is distributed, whether inflation is being taken into account (real versus nominal), the amount spent on investment and long-term socially beneficial projects, and population change. When the total population has changed (if there are more people then the increased income has to be spread out over the greater number) it is better to look at **GDP per capita**.

> **Standard of living** is a measure of the quality of life. The measure can include physical assets and consumption, and less easily measured variables such as happiness, lack of stress, length of hours worked, lack of pollution, and capacity of houses.
>
> **GDP per capita** (per head) is total GDP divided by the population. Total population figures cannot be assumed to be constant when looking at GDP, so GDP per capita gives a better indicator of incomes.

Now test yourself
Tested

2   Does a higher growth rate mean a country is enjoying higher living standards?

Answers on p. 105

Growth in different countries

Revised

An increase in GDP in one country of 10% does not mean that the country is doing better than a country with an increase of 5%. An evaluation of growth figures depends on:

- how well off the country is in the first place
- how much of the output is self-consumed, so does not appear as GDP
- methods of calculation and reliability of data
- relative exchange rates — do they represent the purchasing power of the local currency?
- type of spending by government — is money spent on warfare, or on **quality of life** issues such as education and health?

> **Quality of life** is a measure of living standards which takes into account more than just income (or GDP).

Volume versus value

Revised

An increase in the volume of output does not always mean that there is an increase in the value of output. Volume of output measures the number of items produced, but if these are falling in price (perhaps because lots of countries are producing the same thing) then value might fall even when volume rises.

> **Typical mistake**
>
> Economic growth is a change in the level of real GDP, not GDP itself. Do not give GDP figures on their own — show a percentage change.

Inflation

> **Examiner's tip**
>
> Look out for falling growth levels. If growth rates are falling but still above zero then *levels* of income are still rising, although at a slower rate.

Inflation is a *sustained* rise in the *general* price level. It is a weighted average of spending of all households in a country (that is, general spending). Changes in the **consumer price index** (CPI) are the measure of inflation used for inflation targeting in the UK. The CPI does not include housing costs such as rent payments and mortgage interest repayments. Changes in the **retail price index** (RPI) (also known as the headline rate) include housing costs, and may be used in data for comparison with CPI.

> **Consumer price index (CPI)** is the measure of inflation used for inflation targeting in the UK. It does not include housing costs such as mortgage interest repayments or rent.
>
> **Retail price index (RPI)** is a measure of inflation. It is also known as the headline rate, and includes housing costs.

> **Now test yourself**
>
> Tested
>
> 3 If oil prices go up sharply, is this inflation?
>
> Answer on p. 105

Calculating the rate of inflation

Revised

Inflation is a measure of the increase in the average price level. The price level is the consumer price index, which is a weighted average of things on which people spend their money. Key points to note:

- Inflation is measured in the UK by *changes* in the CPI.
- The CPI is given as an **index number**. This means that it is a number shown as a percentage relative to the **base year**, which is given the value 100.
- Inflation is usually shown on a year to year basis, so you need to calculate the change over original × 100.

> An **index number** is a number shown relative to another number in percentage terms, so the actual figures are removed and just the relative difference is shown.
>
> A **base year** is used for comparison between price levels in different time periods. It is given the number 100.

Households spend different amounts on various items. It is important to incorporate this in the calculation of inflation so that price changes will be fully reflected in the cost of living. In order to find a rate of inflation that represents the changes in costs of living that households experience:

- the *Living Costs and Food Survey* collects information from a sample of nearly 7000 households in the UK using self-reported diaries of all purchases
- **weights** are assigned to each item that is bought by the average household
- the weights show the proportion of income spent on each item
- a price survey is undertaken by civil servants who collect data once a month about changes in the price of the 650 most commonly used goods and services in a variety of retail outlets

The price changes are multiplied by the weights to give a price index; you can measure inflation from this by calculating the percentage change in this index over consecutive years.

Now test yourself
Tested ☐

4 Does the price survey involve looking at just 650 items? If more, why is this?

Answer on p. 105

> **Typical mistake**
>
> What is inflation if the consumer price index changes from 125 to 130? This is an increase of (5/125) times 100, which is an inflation rate of 4% not 5%. Most people divide by 100 rather than the 'original', which is 125.

> **Weights** show the proportion of income spent on items and are used to ensure that the percentage change in price reflects the impact on the average family in terms of their spending.

> **Examiner's tip**
>
> Many students think that the CPI or RPI is inflation. But it is *changes* in these price levels that show inflation.

The significance of inflation
Revised ☐

Inflation is an important measure of the success of an economy, and inflation rates that are too high or too low are a sign that the economy is experiencing problems.

In the UK there is an **inflation target** (currently 2% CPI rises with a permissable range of + or −1%). This means that a rise in the average level of prices of 2% is the desired level.

The government chooses the target and delegates the task of achievement of this goal to an independent body, the **Monetary Policy Committee** (MPC) — see page 98. We say that the MPC implements monetary policy in the UK.

- The MPC is a group of nine Bank of England economists/industrialists/ academic economists who meet monthly to set the **base rate of interest**.
- If inflation rises above 3% (**ceiling**) or goes below 1% (**floor**) then the MPC has failed to reach a target.
- This means that the MPC has to explain its failure to meet the target in an open letter to the government.
- If interest rates are raised then this is a measure intended to reduce the rate of inflation.
- If interest rates are cut then this is a signal that inflation is not a threat to the economy and other aims, such as reflating the economy, might become more important.

The target for inflation in the UK is 2% by the CPI measure, which means the average cost of living will rise by 2%. If earnings rise on average by 2% then on average no one is worse off. But the measure of inflation might

> **Inflation target** — in the UK the government tasks the Monetary Policy Committee with the objective of 2% inflation, within a range of tolerance of plus or minus 1%.
>
> The **base rate of interest** is the tool used primarily in the UK to control the level of inflation. It is the cost of credit that the central bank set for its immediate financial transactions, and other rates of interest in the economy are based pro rata against this.
>
> **Ceiling** and **floor** — if inflation goes above 3% (ceiling) or below 1% (floor) then it means that it is 'off target'.

not be a true representation of the changes in living costs. It does not include housing costs, which are a significant item of expenditure for most households in the UK. Some people do not have representative spending patterns and so might experience cost of living rises of more or less than the average shown by the CPI.

Now test yourself   Tested

5 Give two reasons why the CPI measure might be inaccurate as a measure of the average cost of living in the UK.

6 Cherry gets a 1% pay rise from her employer, but the rate of inflation is 4%. What, to the nearest whole number, happens to her real wage?

Answers on p. 105

Employment and unemployment

Employment   Revised

Employment can be measured as a level (number of people in work) or as a percentage (number of people in work divided by the total number of people who are **economically active**, multiplied by 100).

Economically active — those people who are at work or who are willing to work. Also called the workforce, the term includes unemployed people.

Typical mistake

Most often people confuse economic activity with employment. This is incorrect, because people who are willing to work but cannot find employment are still economically active. Economic inactivity refers to people who are not willing to work, such as students or people caring for other people as unpaid activity, people not of working age and those who are unable to work.

Unemployment   Revised

Unemployment can be measured as a level (number of people looking for work but unable to find it) or as a percentage (number of people out of work divided by the total number of people who are economically active, multiplied by 100).

Types of unemployment

- **Cyclical** (or demand deficient) — where lack of spending in the economy/recession means that people are out of work.
- **Structural** — where industries are in decline and workers' skills are becoming obsolete (out of date).
- **Frictional** — where people are between jobs.
- **Classical** — where there are problems with the supply side of labour, (e.g. the minimum wage is too high).

Costs of unemployment

- Costs to the person without an income.
- Non-income costs to the unemployed person. Skills become obsolete, and people can lose confidence.
- Costs to firms — people don't spend as much in the shops.

- Costs to governments. Governments have to spend more on **Jobseeker's allowance** and they receive less in income tax and other taxes.

> **Jobseeker's allowance (JSA)** is a payment made to people who are willing and able to work but are not currently in employment. When an economy grows, JSA is likely to fall as more people who are willing to work do manage to find work.

Measures of unemployment

The two measures of unemployment used in the UK are:

- The **ILO measure** (conducted by the Labour Force Survey) uses a questionnaire to ask people aged 16–65 whether they have been out of work over the last four weeks and are ready to start within two weeks.
- The **Claimant Count** records people who have successfully claimed Jobseeker's allowance (JSA).

Revision activity

Visit the BBC news website and find 'economy tracker'. Look at the measures of success of the UK economy according to these measures. Make a note of key figures such as the employment and unemployment rates, which you might refer to in your exam.

Now test yourself

Tested

7 If you add together the percentage of the population employed with the percentage unemployed you will only get to around 80% of the population in the UK. What is the other 20% doing?

8 Why might the ILO measure be higher than the Claimant Count measure?

9 Why might the Claimant Count rise relative to the ILO measure of unemployment?

Answers on p. 105

Benefits of increased employment

Revised

For increases in employment, the benefits might include:

- **Increased incomes** — with rises in standards of living for households
- **Improved skills (human capital)** of workers.
- **Multiplier effects** — as increased incomes lead to increased spending, so firms might see increased profits.
- **Higher government taxation revenue** and falling spending on JSA.

> **Human capital** is the education and skills that a workforce possesses. Investment in people has a value.

Revision activity

Using the reverse of the arguments for increasing employment, explain the costs of decreasing employment. Are these the same as the costs of increasing unemployment?

Migration and employment/unemployment

Revised

Migration may occur when people:

- are searching for work or better paid work
- study abroad
- escape from social or political problems in their original country
- accompany family members
- disagree with tax structures
- wish to 'get away from' or 'get to' people or places

The economic implications for employment and unemployment depend largely on the reasons for both **immigration** and **emigration**.

> **Migration** is a general term that looks at both immigration, emigration and the overall balance between the two in a country (net migration).
> **Immigration** is when people enter a country for long-term stay.
> **Emigration** is when people exit a country for long-term stay.

- If immigrants come into a country to fill vacancies then immigration leads to an increase in employment.
- But if immigrants are looking for work and either do not find it or displace other people from work then employment may be unchanged and unemployment might increase.

Revision activity

Think of one reason why each of the reasons for migration might increase both employment and unemployment. For example, people looking for work might find jobs that people in the UK cannot fill (increased employment of, say, doctors) and might increase unemployment (immigrants finding work might displace people currently working in the UK).

Typical mistake

Most people assume that migration entails cost to the government. Remember that employed immigrants pay tax to the UK government, increasing government revenue, and improve human capital.

Now test yourself

Tested ☐

10 If immigrants come into the UK for full-time study, what will happen to the level of employment and unemployment?

Answer on p. 105

Balance of payments

The **balance of payments** is a record of international payments over the course of a year.

The **balance of payments** is a record of international payments over the course of a year.

The current account

Revised ☐

The current account records payments for transactions in the present year (other than investments or speculation) and comprises:

- trade in goods
- trade in services
- investment income (interest, profit and dividends) and
- transfers (e.g. tax payments to foreign governments)

Capital account and financial account: these accounts relate to other parts of the balance of payments (investment and speculation) that you do not need to know for the AS exam.

Typical mistake

The investment income on the current account is not the flow of investment funds, which do not feature on the current account. Investment income is the reward for investment which is paid in the current period.

Typical mistake

Imports are not a flow in but a *flow out* of money from a country. If I go on holiday in a foreign country then this is recorded as an import, because money is flowing out of the UK.

Current account deficit

Revised ☐

Causes of a **current account deficit** might include:

- the currency is too strong relative to other countries (e.g. if the pound buys many euros then people holding euros will not want to buy goods and services from the UK and people in the UK will be keen to buy things from the euro area)
- high rates of inflation relative to other countries
- high wage costs relative to other countries
- high level of growth in a country, meaning people with higher incomes tend to buy more imports from abroad

A **current account deficit** on the balance of payments occurs when more money is flowing out of the country than is flowing in on the current account.

Exam practice answers and quick quizzes at **www.hodderplus.co.uk/myrevisionnotes**

Current account surplus

Causes of a **current account surplus** might include:

- the currency is too weak relative to other countries (e.g. if the Chinese renminbi buys many US dollars then people holding renminbi will not want to buy goods and services from the rest of the world and people in China will find it difficult to buy things from outside China)
- low rates of inflation relative to other countries
- low wage costs relative to other countries
- low level of growth in a country, making it difficult to buy imports from abroad and creating a strong incentive for firms in the country to export

> A **current account surplus** of the balance of payments occurs when more money is flowing into the country than is flowing out.

> **Revision activity**
> Make a list of the countries with the largest current account deficits and surpluses. These are usually listed in a table in Wikipedia.

Now test yourself

Tested

11 You go to Spain for a holiday. Is this an export or an import on the UK's balance of payments?

Answer on p. 105

Measures of development

The human development index

The **human development index** (HDI) is a **composite measure** of quality of life which is valuable for comparing living standards in different countries. It overcomes some of the problems of using income alone, by taking into account education (years of schooling) and health (life expectancy) along with incomes per head adjusted to **purchasing power parity** (PPP).

> **Human development index** is a composite measure of quality of life which has one third weighting for education, one third for health and one third for GDP per head at purchasing power parity.

> **Composite measure** — a measure that is made up of a combination of other measures.

> **Purchasing power parity** — when values of income are expressed at PPP it means that the exchange rate used is the one where the same basket of goods in the country could be bought in the USA at this rate of currency exchange.

Now test yourself

Tested

12 If a hamburger costs $3 in the USA and 30 Sri Lankan rupees what is the PPP exchange rate?

13 If the actual US dollar to Sri Lanka rupee exchange rate is $1 = 130 Sri Lankan rupees, is the rupee over or under-valued, and what does this mean?

Answers on p. 105

Other measures of development

Other measures apart from HDI are useful for measuring standards of living, especially when a variety of measures are used together.

- HDI does not give a strong indication of how living standards might change in the future.
- HDI does not indicate deprivation: that is, what people are going without, such as water.
- HDI is not clear on poverty lines and how difficult life might be for some people.
- Other measures might be useful in conjunction with GDP or HDI to give a broader picture of how well a country is developing.

- A helpful figure is the percentage of adult male labour in agriculture. The classification is made narrow and precise (adult and male) to make comparisons safer across different customs. The higher the number of employees involved in agriculture then in general the opportunities for development are weaker.

- Likewise, the higher the levels of access to clean water, the greater the likelihood of increased life expectancies in the future.

Exam practice

Extract 1 Changes to the composition of the basket of goods

Apple iPads and Samsung Galaxy tablets have been added to the basket of goods used to measure how quickly consumer prices are rising, as have teen novels, baby wipes and chicken and chips takeaways from fast-food outlets, according to the government body that compiles official inflation rates. The growing popularity of tablet devices made them suitable for addition in their own right for 2012. 'Chicken and chips' was being added because that type of product was under-represented, perhaps because cash-strapped Britons are consuming more cheap and easy meals at a time of high food prices.

The removal of prices for processing colour film reflects the growing use of digital cameras.

Source: adapted from the Office for National Statistics (ONS)

Questions

1 With reference to the article, explain why items get added and removed from the 'basket'. [4]

2 Why does it matter what is in the 'basket' and the proportion spent on each item? [8]

3 Very few pensioners currently use tablet-device computers. Explain why this might cause a problem for a government in the process of setting the annual change in pension allowance. [6]

Answers and quick quizzes online

Online

Examiner's summary

✔ Economic growth measures increases in real GDP or increases in potential capacity in an economy. It can lead to an increase in living standards, but this is not guaranteed, and many other factors are also required for an improvement in welfare.

✔ Controlling inflation is another of the six main objectives of governments. In the UK there is a target of 2%. The task of controlling inflation is the responsibility of the Monetary Policy Committee (MPC) in the UK. It raises interest rates to try to cut inflation, and cuts interest rates if inflation is low to allow other areas of the economy to improve.

✔ Employment and unemployment are not opposites, but different ways of looking at the efficiency in the use of the country's workforce.

✔ The balance of payments is another way to judge the health of an economy, by looking at flows of money in and out of the country. Exports bring money flows into a country, and imports see money flowing out.

✔ The human development index (HDI) is a much broader measure of the development of an economy, taking into account incomes per head at purchasing power parity (one third weight), years of schooling expected and received (one third weight) and life expectancy (one third weight). Other measures of development can be used to add further aspects of economic development in various countries.

7 Income and wealth, aggregate demand, aggregate supply and equilibrium

Income, wealth, injections and withdrawals

National income Revised

National income is the amount received by various agents in an economy, by households, firms and government.

- It is the same as GDP (gross domestic product) measured by households, firms and government.
- It is the same as total spending by households, firms and government.
- This assumes that **leakages** — which are savings, tax and imports — and injections — which are investment, government spending and exports — have been taken into account.

National income is a flow of money: that is, a movement of money from one person to another, rather than a stock of money such as savings in a bank, physical **assets** such as buildings, or shares. The stock of assets in an economy is called **wealth**.

> **Leakages** are an outflow from the circular flow of money. These comprise saving, taxation, and the money spent on imports. Also known as 'withdrawals'.
>
> An **asset** is an accumulation of wealth; factors which can be used to provide income in the future. It is also called capital stock.
>
> **Wealth** is a stock of assets (e.g. valuable factories).

Income and wealth Revised

There is a strong **correlation** between **income** and wealth. The ownership of wealth in itself can mean that there are interest payments or rent. When wealth changes in value (e.g. house prices rise or fall) there is an impact on people's spending and therefore incomes. For example, if my house is worth more than I paid for it, I might feel more confident about buying a new car and the bank manager might lend me the money because he is confident that my house can act as **collateral**.

> **Income** is a flow of money (e.g. wages).
>
> **Collateral assets** are used as security for a loan.

The circular flow of income

Revised

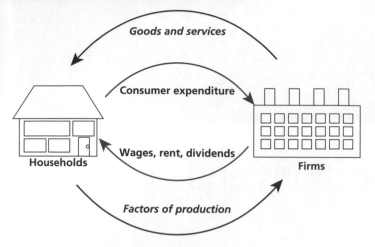

Figure 7.1 The circular flow of income (income is shown in red)

Changes to the flow of income (see Figure 7.1) occur when there is a change in one of the three **injections** into the circular flow of income. The injections are:

- I — investment: an increase in the capital stock (assets).
- G — government spending: where the government buys goods and services such as health care in the NHS.
- X — exports: where people from abroad buy domestically produced goods and services.

Investment is an increase in spending when capital assets are bought as well as consumer items. So for example, if a firm buys a new machine, there is more spending in the economy because the machine has to be made, which in turn means a greater number of incomes.

Injections are an input into the circular flow of money. These inputs comprise investment, government spending and export income.

Typical mistake

Saving is not the same as investment; in fact the two are complete opposites. Saving represents a decrease in the amount of spending in the economy as we forgo current spending for future spending.

Now test yourself

1 If the government decreases its spending on defence, what will happen to the total amount of spending in an economy?

Answer on p. 105

Tested

Aggregate demand

What is aggregate demand?

Revised

Aggregate demand (AD) is the total amount of planned spending on goods and services at any price level in an economy.

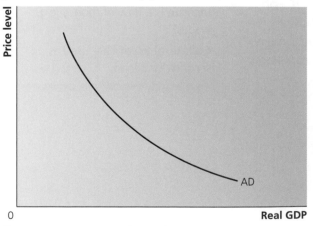

Figure 7.2 An aggregate demand curve

Exam practice answers and quick quizzes at **www.hodderplus.co.uk/myrevisionnotes**

Important features about the aggregate demand curve:

- This diagram (see Figure 7.2) can be drawn as a straight line or a curve.
- Aggregate demand shows that as the general price level falls, national income, output or spending will increase.

There are three main reasons why aggregate demand slopes downwards:

- The **real balance effect**: a decrease in the price level increases the real value of money. The larger the quantity of real money, the larger the quantity of goods and services demanded.
- The **international trade effect**: if UK goods become cheaper then, ceteris paribus, UK citizens will buy more UK goods (a fall in imports) and foreigners will buy more UK goods (an increase in exports).
- The **substitution effect** over time: for various reasons, a fall in the average price level means there are lower interest rates. This means there is a shift in aggregate demand from the *future* to the *present*, so increasing the quantity of goods demanded today.

Revision activity

Explain to a friend why the AD curve is downward sloping using your normal language and avoiding any economics jargon. Remember that just saying 'prices are lower so we buy more' is not correct.

Examiner's tip

It does not make any difference to your mark whether you draw AD as a straight line or a curve. Choose the method that you feel most comfortable with.

The components of aggregate demand

Revised

Aggregate demand is made up of the following components:

$$C + I + G + (X - M)$$

Consumption (C)

This is spending by households on goods and services, and it is the main component of AD (about 65%). For example, it records how much you spend on food and clothes. The main determinants of consumption are as follows.

- **Interest rate (the cost of credit).** If **interest rates** rise then it costs us more to borrow if we are going to spend on credit and it increases the opportunity cost of spending (i.e. saving); higher interest rates mean that more money can be earned by leaving money in the bank.
- **Consumer confidence.** If households feel secure in their jobs and future prospects for the economy, then they are more likely to buy big-ticket items such as new cars or expensive electrical goods. Because of this, what people think is going to happen to the economy has a big influence on what actually does happen.
- **Wealth effects.** An increase in share or house prices means that households are willing and able to spend more (e.g. if my house is worth more I might take out a larger loan on my house, and if my shares go up in value I might be more willing to book a foreign holiday, even if I do not in fact sell my house or my shares).
- **The level of employment and wage rates.** The higher the level of employment, the more will be spent in a country (which might lead to even higher employment).

Examiner's tip

Economists us 'M' as an abbreviation for imports because 'I' is used for investment. You can use the X and M abbreviations in the exam.

The **interest rate** is the cost of credit (borrowing) or the reward for saving.

The **wealth effect** is the effect on spending or incomes when asset prices change.

Now test yourself

Tested

2   If interest rates fall what will happen to consumption?

Answer on p. 105

Investment (I)

Investment is defined as increase in the capital stock. The main influences are:

- **Interest rates.** If interest rates rise, investment tends to fall because it costs more to borrow the money in order to invest.
- **Confidence levels.** If firms think that they will sell more in the future they are more likely to invest today.
- **Risk.** The higher the level of risk, the lower the level of investment.
- **Government decisions.** If the government decides to cut **corporation tax** (a tax on profit) then firms are more likely to invest.
- **Government bureaucracy.** If the government relaxes planning restrictions — as they have done recently with buildings in the UK — firms are more likely to invest in building projects.

Government expenditure (G)

Governments can choose to some extent how much they spend and deliberately manipulate total spending in the economy by changing their own level of spending. This is called **discretionary fiscal policy**.

- The government does not have to 'balance its books' in the short run, meaning that it can spend more or less than it earns in taxation.
- If the government spends *more* than it earns, this is known as a **fiscal or budget deficit**; this will increase the flow of income, or AD.
- If the government spends *less* than it earns, this is known as a **fiscal or budget surplus** and leads to a contraction of aggregate demand (AD). We will look at fiscal policy in Chapter 10.

Exports minus imports (X – M), or net exports

This is the last component of aggregate demand. In the UK this is a negative figure, meaning that the outflow of money for foreign goods and services is greater than the inflow that the UK receives from its exports.

The causes of changes in **net exports** are:

- **Change in exchange rate.** If the **exchange rate** rises, net exports are likely to fall as exports become less competitive and imports become more competitive in the domestic economy. However, in the short run a strong exchange rate might increase the value of exports and decrease the value of imports, as spending patterns do not adjust quickly to price changes. This is known as low price elasticity of demand for exports and imports. It causes the opposite reaction to AD than the one normally expected, as people take time to adjust their spending.
- **Changes in the state of the world economy.** The value of UK exports is heavily dependent on growth rates around the world. The slowdown in the Eurozone has caused UK exports to fall, especially to Spain. The crisis in the Eurozone has meant that spending on Chinese imports has been dramatically reduced, causing Chinese growth rates to fall because China is heavily dependent on exports to the Eurozone.

Corporation tax is a tax on profits that firms make. This tax affects the level of investment that firms make (aggregate demand) and it also affects the amount that firms are willing to supply at any price level (that is, aggregate supply).

Government bureaucracy is the level of government regulations and paperwork that is required to make any business decisions.

Examiner's tip

Do not confuse interest rates with inflation. Interest rates may be used to control inflation and inflation can erode real interest rates, but otherwise they are very different concepts.

Fiscal policy is the government's position or set of decisions on government spending and taxation.

Examiner's tip

Examiners tend to use the words 'budget' and 'fiscal' to mean the same thing. So do not be alarmed if you are asked to explain a budget or fiscal deficit — your answer will be the same. It means that the government is spending more than it is receiving in taxation.

Net exports — the export of goods and services means that money flows into a country; when the value of the money flowing out of the country (as imports) is deducted, a figure for net exports is the result.

The **exchange rate** is the price of one currency in terms of another.

- **Non-price factors.** Demand for exports and imports is determined by many things apart from price, such as quality of engineering, reliability of after-sales service, tariffs and transport costs.

Examiner's tip

If our currency gets stronger it means it can buy more of a foreign currency, so our imports are cheaper and exports cost more to people abroad. Many candidates get confused by this in the exam, and the best way to remember it is to use the mnemonic SPICED — 'strong pound, imports cheap, exports dear' (if you know that 'dear' is another word for expensive).

Now test yourself

3 Does a fall in the currency value increase or decrease aggregate demand?

Answer on p. 105

Tested ☐

The AD curve

Revised ☐

A movement along the AD curve

- This occurs when there is a change in the price level caused by factors that are not related to aggregate demand, i.e. changes in aggregate supply.
- For example, a fall in oil prices (causing a decrease in the cost of production for all firms) would result in a expansion in AD and a fall in the price level, as shown in Figure 7.3.

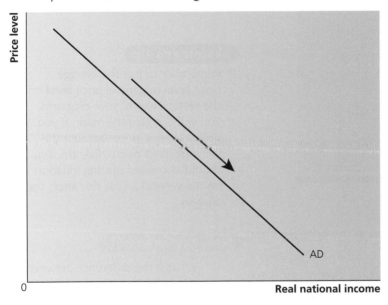

Figure 7.3 Expansion in aggregate demand

Shifts of the AD curve

Aggregate demand shifts when any one of the components C + I + G + (X – M) changes (see Figures 7.4 and 7.5). The analysis above (pp. 73–75) explains why they might change. The size of the change depends on the multiplier effect (see page 80).

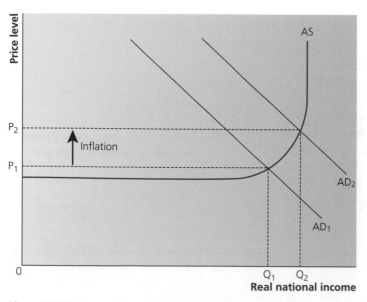

Figure 7.4 An increase in aggregate demand

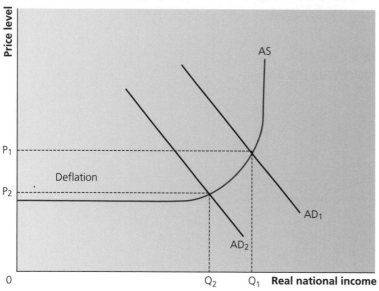

Figure 7.5 A decrease in aggregate demand

Examiner's tip

Remember to put the average price **level** or general price **level** on the vertical axis of your diagrams. You will not gain the marks if you simple label it 'price' because this will look like a micro diagram. You should also avoid putting inflation on the vertical axis as this alters the analysis.

When aggregate demand shifts there will be changes in the price level and equilibrium real output.

- If aggregate demand increases we expect the average level of prices to rise (inflation) and real output to increase (economic growth).

- If aggregate demand decreases we expect the average level of prices to fall (deflation or falling prices) and real output to decrease (slowdown or recession).

Now test yourself

4   What is the difference between a movement along the AD curve and a shift?

Answer on p. 105

Tested

Aggregate supply

What is aggregate supply?   Revised

Aggregate supply is the amount that all firms in the economy are willing to supply at various price levels.

- It is based on the costs of production and incorporates rent, wages, interest and profits.

- As prices rise, firms are generally willing to supply more but there comes a point where firms reach maximum capacity which we will call full employment (at Y_f in Figure 7.6).

- You can draw AS as a straight line sloping upwards to indicate that there are rising costs as firms try to produce more.
- Or you can show AS with a horizontal section where there is spare capacity, an upward sloping part where there are bottlenecks in the economy, and a vertical part at full employment.

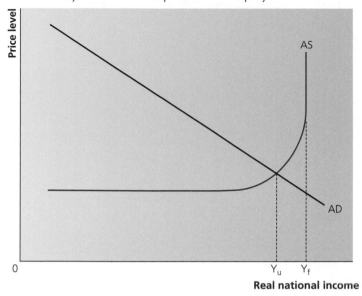

Figure 7.6 Aggregate supply

If the costs of production rise, the aggregate supply shifts up/left. For example:

- if the price of oil rises, firms will not be willing to supply unless they can receive more money for the same output
- if investment falls, for example because interest rates have risen, then again aggregate supply decreases
- if there is a shortage of certain factors of production, for example skilled labour, then this will raise costs for firms

If an economy can increase output without significant increase in costs (that is, the aggregate supply is not vertical), we say there is **spare capacity** (or an output gap, see page 82). This means there are unused resources in the economy, meaning some unemployment (at Y_U in Figure 7.6).

- The Keynesian view is that there can be equilibrium in an economy and also spare capacity.
- The argument is that you cannot leave unemployment and recession to disappear by themselves as market forces force prices down and make the resources more employable.

Approaches to aggregate supply

The **Keynesian approach** to aggregate supply reflects the belief that an economy can be at equilibrium when there is spare capacity in the economy.

The **classical approach** to aggregate supply reflects the view that if there is spare capacity in the economy it cannot be said to be at equilibrium and eventually the spare capacity will disappear. That is, the aggregate supply is vertical in the long run.

Spare capacity is where there are unemployed resources in an economy.

The **Keynesian approach** is the view that there can be equilibrium unemployment, and governments can take action to stimulate aggregate demand to achieve long-term growth and employment.

The **classical approach** is the view that markets work best if left to themselves. If there is unemployment then labour markets should be left to themselves. Wages will fall until people can find work.

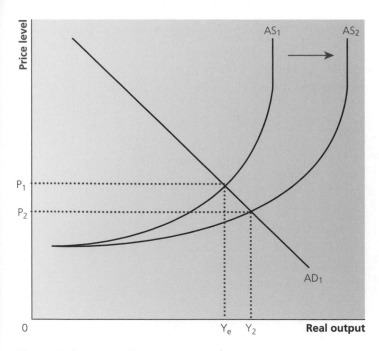

Figure 7.7 An increase in aggregate supply

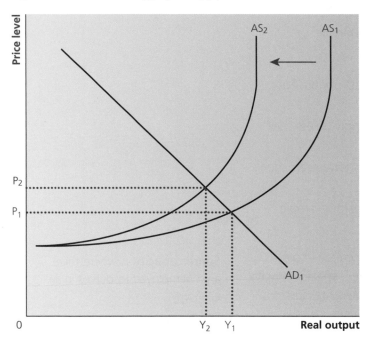

Figure 7.8 An decrease in aggregate supply

Movements along the aggregate supply curve occur when aggregate demand shifts and the price level changes (see Figures 7.7 and 7.8).

● So if there is an increase in aggregate demand, aggregate supply will expand and firms will produce more.

● So if there is a decrease in aggregate demand, aggregate supply will contract and firms will produce less.

Now test yourself   Tested ☐

5   Why do AS curves sometimes get drawn as a backwards-facing L-shape?

Answer on p. 105

Examiner's tip

It is probably worth drawing the AS curve as a curve rather than a straight line. This will make it easier for you to talk about output gaps and other Keynesian analysis. It will also make it easier for you to evaluate, as you can discuss where the AD crosses the AS and the differing impact of the price level on real output that results.

Why does aggregate supply shift?

There are many changes that might make firms willing to supply more or less at any given price level. If costs to firms decrease we say that there is an increase in aggregate supply, and if costs to firms increase we say that there is a decrease in aggregate supply.

The following factors might cause a shift in aggregate supply.

- **Changing costs of raw materials.** If the cost of oil rises, the cost of production of almost everything will rise, meaning that aggregate supply decreases (shifts to the left or upwards).
- **Change in the level of international trade.** For example, if trade is inhibited by a new tax on imports (a tariff), costs for domestic firms tend to rise as they cannot enjoy low production costs using cheap raw materials.
- **Change in exchange rates.** If the pound gets stronger, imports become cheaper and aggregate supply increases (shifts down or to the right).
- **Technological advances.** For example, new computer-aided technology can reduce costs for a broad range of firms.
- **Relative productivity changes.** Productivity is defined as output per unit of input. So if there is an improvement in the industry, and workflow becomes more efficient, then AS shifts down or to the right.
- **Education skills changes.** If more people are well educated then aggregate supply increases.
- **Regulation changes.** If the government makes new laws to make it easier to set up and run businesses then aggregate supply increases (shifts right or down). This is sometimes called a cut in red tape or cut in bureaucracy.
- **Changes in the minimum wage.** Increases in the minimum wage can increase costs for firms, meaning that aggregate supply falls. However, there is evidence that increasing minimum wages can increase the productivity of workers, which might mean that aggregate supply increases.
- **Changes in the tax and benefit system.** A cut in taxes on firms might increase aggregate supply. A cut in benefits might make people more desperate to keep their jobs or to find work, meaning productivity increases — although it might mean that people are less healthy, or less able to concentrate at work.

Now test yourself

6   Will an increase in the interest rate cause aggregate supply to increase or decrease?

Answer on p. 106

Typical mistake

Most candidates shift AS the wrong way. Remember than an increase in AS makes it shift right or down. This sounds a bit odd. But it is because when there is an increase, the *output* increases at any particular price level.

Examiner's tip

When you are trying to decide whether there will be a change in AD or AS, remember that AS is the firms' perspective. Think about costs of production.

Equilibrium — putting AD and AS together

Equilibrium

Revised

When aggregate demand meets aggregate supply there is an **equilibrium** point, which tells us the price level and real GDP of a country (see Figure 7.9).

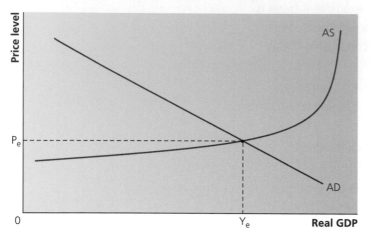

Figure 7.9 Equilibrium

> An **equilibrium** is a balancing point where there is no tendency to change.

An equilibrium is a balancing point where there is no tendency to change the price level or output level.

- If prices were higher than the balancing point P_e, there would be a tendency for them to fall because supply would be greater than demand and there would be lots of unsold goods and services.
- If prices were lower than the balancing point, there would be shortages and prices would start to rise in order to make sure that everyone could get what they were prepared to pay for.
- If, for example, a world-wide recession and a fall in aggregate demand occurred, you would expect to see falls in prices (or that prices did not rise very quickly).

Now test yourself

Tested

7 Is equilibrium a good thing?

Answer on p. 106

The multiplier

Revised

The **multiplier** shows the amount by which a change in an injection or leakage causes total spending to change. It is the result of income being re-spent in the economy, having **second and successive round effects**.

If the injections into the circular flow increase then there will be a larger final change on total spending in the economy. The multiplier times the injection gives the final change to spending.

> **Positive multiplier effect** — the amount by which an increase in spending produces an increase in total spending in the economy.
>
> **Second round effects** — changes when firms, individuals and governments respond to initial changes.

Exam practice answers and quick quizzes at **www.hodderplus.co.uk/myrevisionnotes**

If the leakages from the circular flow increase then the multiplier effect will be smaller. For example, when the 2008 recession hit the UK, the saving ratio rose markedly, reducing the multiplier effect.

Now test yourself

Tested

8 If there is an injection of £1 million into an economy and the multiplier is 2, what is the total change in spending in the economy?

Answer on p. 106

Why is the multiplier important?

If there is a change in any one of the injections or leakages, the total effect on the economy as a whole will be much greater than the original change. So the multiplier magnifies the impact of changes on the economy as a whole. The larger the multiplier, the greater the impact of any changes in injections or leakages.

Revision activity

Write the list of three injections and three leakages, then check you have identified them all from pages 71–72.

Exam practice

Discuss the likely impact on aggregate demand when there is an increase in the value of the currency. [30]

Answer and quick quizzes online

Online

Examiner's summary

✔ The main piece of analysis in macroeconomics, and the building block for most of the conclusions you will need to reach, can be found in aggregate demand and supply analysis.

✔ Aggregate demand: there are forces which determine how much people in an economy are prepared to buy at any price level, and the agents of this demand are consumers, firms, the government and foreign purchasers of our exports. We take off the value of imports and use the formula AD = C + I + G + (X − M).

✔ Aggregate supply: the amount that firms are willing to supply at any price level. The higher the prices that can be charged, the more firms are willing to supply.

The curve shifts when there are changes in costs that affect all firms, such as changes in oil prices, taxes or productivity of workers.

✔ Putting aggregate demand and supply together, we get an equilibrium price level and output, which tells us what inflation and growth will be as AS or AD shifts. The causes of these shifts will be examined in your exam, and you should remember that changes in determinants of aggregate demand are magnified by the working of the multiplier. This is the impact of incomes being re-spent in an economy, so any change in spending has second and subsequent round effects.

8 Economic growth: causes, constraints, benefits and costs

Actual and potential growth, causes and constraints

Economic growth

Revised

Economists have two very different meanings for the term 'economic growth':

1 **Actual growth** is the measure of changes in **real GDP**, measured by adding up all the incomes in the country, or all the spending, or all the output. Although none of these measures is entirely reliable, between them we do get a good indication of the changes of activity in the economy.

2 **Potential growth**, probably a more important measure than actual growth, which shows how much the economy could produce if all the resources were being used. It is useful for measuring the success of governments and assessing the likelihood of changes in living standards over time.

The difference between the two is the output gap, and the bigger the output gap, the more the economy is inefficient in its use of resources. In fact a persistent **output gap** tends to lead to a fall in potential output.

Output gaps are a sign that the country is not using its resources efficiently, or at their maximum potential. They are formed for a variety of reasons:

- resources available are not suited to the needs of the economy
- the welfare system pays generously for some people not to work
- the effects of relocation of production to other countries
- increased competitiveness of other countries
- structural changes, meaning the economy no longer produces output that is tailored to the needs of the market (e.g. ship building when the government decides to cut back on the size of the navy)

Sustainable growth is the highest rate of growth which does not compromise the ability of an economy to grow in the future. For example, if an economy grows very quickly by mining all its resources, it might find it difficult to grow in the future.

> **Actual growth** is the increase in real GDP.
>
> **Real GDP** is the output of an economy, with the effects of inflation removed.
>
> **Potential growth** is the amount by which a country could increase its production if all resources were used efficiently.
>
> The **output gap** is the difference between actual GDP (or growth) and potential GDP (or growth).

> **Typical mistake**
>
> A falling rate of growth does not mean that real GDP is falling. If it is still positive, then a falling rate of growth means that incomes are rising, albeit more slowly.

> **Examiner's tip**
>
> There are many ways to draw an output gap on a diagram. Make sure that you are confident in at least one of these ways, for example in drawing a PPF curve where the point of output is not on the PPF but inside the curve.

Now test yourself

Tested

1 If growth rates change from 3.2% to 2.0%, what has happened to the level of real GDP?

Answer on p. 106

Causes of growth

Growth occurs when there is an increase in aggregate demand or aggregate supply, meaning that there is a new equilibrium output at a level where more is produced.

- It occurs with multiplier effects when there is a shift in aggregate demand.
- If the aggregate supply curve is vertical then when aggregate demand shifts there will *not* be growth — in other words, actual growth cannot occur beyond full capacity.

Aggregate demand shifts

Aggregate demand increases when something causes any of the components to increase.

Here is a list of possible causes of increases but many more are possible.

1 Increase in consumption (C)

- Cut in the interest rate, meaning the opportunity cost of saving falls, and the cost of borrowing to invest falls. It can also lead to falls in the cost of mortgage interest repayments, so people have more money left to spend on other things in the economy.
- Increase in confidence.
- Wealth effects from rising house or share prices.

> **Typical mistake**
>
> Consumption is a measure of the spending on goods and services in an economy. It is neither an injection nor a leakage, but a measure of the flow of income in an economy.

2 Increase in investment (I)

- Firms invest more when the cost of borrowing falls (interest rate cut).
- Increase in confidence of firms. If firms think there will be growth they are more likely to invest, which in itself is likely to stimulate growth.

> **Typical mistake**
>
> Investment is *not* saving in a bank. Investment is an increase in capital assets, for example buying a machine.

3 Increase in government spending (G)

Governments can use fiscal policy to stimulate the economy. This means spending on government projects such as health and education when the rest of the economy is lacking in aggregate demand. Note that this is a Keynesian policy and that classical economists argue that it will only cause inflation or debt.

4 Increase in net exports (X – M)

Economies can be stimulated through export-led growth. China and Germany notably sailed through the last recession by maintaining spending through exports. In order to stimulate exports the following strategies might be successful.

- Hold the exchange rate down (as in China holding their currency, the renminbi, down). This makes exports relatively cheap and imports relatively expensive. However, in the UK we have a freely floating exchange rate and no manipulation is possible.
- Reduce tariffs and quotas. Encouraging trade tends to lead to an improvement in exports in the long run, but the initial effect is often an increase in imports, which actually reduces AD.
- Encourage productivity and efficiency in export markets. The problem is that this is really a supply-side policy but it has an impact on the aggregate demand side.

> **Typical mistake**
>
> Many students get confused about the impact of imports on aggregate demand. Remember that when a country imports goods or products that means that money is flowing out, so a rise in imports means that more money is leaving the country. This means there is less spending within this country: that is, there is a fall in aggregate demand.

Aggregate supply shifts

Shifting AS to the right or down comes under the category of supply-side policies. These tend to be long run and involve governments enabling firms to produce more at lower costs.

The types of policy that may be used are as follows.

● Cutting corporation taxes (taxes on profits) so that firms have a strong incentive to produce more.

● Removing regulations and other restrictions preventing firms from growing (e.g. removing restrictions on mergers to allow these to take place).

● Encouraging investment by forcing banks to lend money, or by easing the credit situation (quantitative easing), or even just cutting the interest rate.

● Increasing the competition in markets. Note that this might conflict with bullet point 2 (deregulation) and allowing more monopolies.

● Privatising or subsidising industries (e.g. the Royal Mail).

● Improving the labour market by increasing educational standards.

● Productivity might increase by spending on the NHS; for example if waiting lists are shorter people can get back to work more promptly (e.g. a cycle courier with a broken leg).

● Improved **incentives** for workers by cutting income tax rates and cutting benefits for out-of-work members of the labour force.

● Improving **infrastructure** (e.g. the UK transport system; internet coverage).

● Measures to make imports cheaper, such as cutting tariffs, mean that for many firms production costs will fall. This is especially significant in the UK as the economy relies heavily on imported raw materials.

> An **incentive** is a factor that makes the labour resource more effective. It might be higher pay for working harder, or more profits if businesses are run successfully.
>
> **Infrastructure** is the capital assets that enable resources to move and be moved, for example motorways and internet connections.

Examiner's tip

Note that cutting interest rates can lead to increases in AD and AS.

Now test yourself

2 What happens to growth if there is an increase in investment?

Answer on p. 106

Tested

Constraints on growth

Constraints on growth are factors that prevent economies from growing. In many contexts you will be able to define these constraints as 'absence of causes of growth' and use the factors listed above under 'aggregate supply shifts'. The following are other factors which might be used.

● lack of **investment** funds or cash to run businesses

● weak or obstructive governments

● currency instability or a **fixed exchange rate** or exchange rates too high

● lack of human capital

● private or public sector debt: the need to pay off or 'service' borrowing in the past can prevent economies spending and investing in the current or future periods

● lack of access to international trade, or a high level of **tariffs** and other forms of protectionism.

> **Investment** is an increase in the capital stock.
>
> A **fixed exchange rate** occurs when governments prevent their currencies from moving with market forces. This can be achieved by legislation or through buying and selling currencies to maintain a certain rate.
>
> A **tariff** is a tax on imports that can prevent growth if it means that firms cannot acquire raw materials or capital goods.

Now test yourself

Tested

3 Why are high exchange rates sometimes viewed as a constraint on growth?

Answer on p. 106

Benefits and costs of growth

Benefits of growth
Revised

- **Increased incomes and standards of living.** Total income for the country is increasing when there is economic growth, and as long as inflation is not increasing at the same rate at least some people will be better off. However, the distribution of income is likely to change and while some people might not be any better off, the gap between them and others might increase.

- **Firms are likely to experience increased profits** when there is increased growth. This is likely to mean that they can make more profits and shareholders can enjoy increased returns. However, firms making inferior goods — that is, where demand falls when income rises — are likely to suffer. For example, lower-end food suppliers or pound shops tend to fare less well in a period of economic growth.

- **Governments benefit in a boom** because more people are working and paying tax and fewer people need benefits such as jobseeker's allowance (JSA), and so we expect there to be a fiscal improvement in a boom. However, many governments see a period of economic growth as a time to reduce income inequalities, which become more apparent as top-end incomes tend to rise faster.

> **Examiner's tip**
> Inferior goods feature in Unit 1 and will not be examined directly in Unit 2, but you can refer to them when discussing the impact of growth on some companies where demand falls when consumers have increased income.

Costs of growth
Revised

Damage to the environment

Damage to the environment can occur, for example, through increased carbon emissions. The by-product of most industrial production is CO_2 and this has an impact on the ozone layer, acid rain and asthma. Growth also causes a rise in fuel emissions (because a greater number of people are travelling to work or travelling to a holiday destination at home or abroad).

Evaluation: Higher incomes can in fact mean that there is more money to clear up environmental damage: catalytic converters can be fitted to cars; firms can be forced to use a certain percentage of bio-fuels or renewable energy; there is money available for investment in new machinery; and firms and governments can be compelled to adopt carbon-offset schemes, or invest in 'green' technology.

Balance of payments problems

Higher incomes mean that people can afford to import more, and firms' need to export is now no longer so pressing as higher profit margins can be made through selling at home rather than abroad. So X falls, M rises and the balance of payments worsens.

Evaluation: If growth is caused by increasing exports, however, then an improvement of the balance of payments is expected. For example, in the EU in 2012 Germany has the highest rate of growth, but also a balance of payments surplus. This is called **export-led growth**.

> **Examiner's tip**
> Remember that an increase in income makes individuals and firms better off, but the country as a whole is worse off if the extra income is used to buy more from abroad.

> **Export-led growth** occurs when the country grows mainly through increasing exports.

Widening income distribution

The **distribution of income** is a measure of the difference in incomes between different groups in an economy. These groups can be measured in a variety of ways, but one common way is to compare the highest 10% of income earners with the lowest **decile.**

> A **decile** is a 10% chunk of an ordered set of data.

When the economy grows it tends to be those who already have a good job who reap the benefits of growth. For example, the manager or shareholders of a business will enjoy the increased profits, whereas other employees (e.g. cleaners or factory workers) are not likely to see dividends which relate to profits.

Evaluation: With continued growth, workers may lobby for higher income and the rewards may trickle down to those on the lower rungs of the pay scale, especially if there is a shortage of labour and these workers cannot be replaced by machinery. The higher the appropriate skill level, the more likely they are to benefit.

> **Examiner's tip**
>
> When a country gets richer overall, there is likely to be a bigger gap between rich and poor.

The opportunity cost of growth

In choosing to achieve economic growth, an economy has to give up other objectives. For example, a country could give more foreign aid, or improve the welfare of pensioners through more generous state aid. These transfer payments are not recorded as growth but may have greater value in terms of improved standards of living.

Evaluation: The opportunity cost of growth is very hard to measure, as we cannot fully know what would have happened if another policy had been used.

> **Now test yourself**
>
> 4 If economic growth makes someone's income rise so that she buys a brand new BMW car from Germany, what are the costs and benefits?
>
> Answer on p. 106
>
> Tested ☐

> **Exam practice**
>
> The growth rate in China is shown in Figure 8.1.
>
>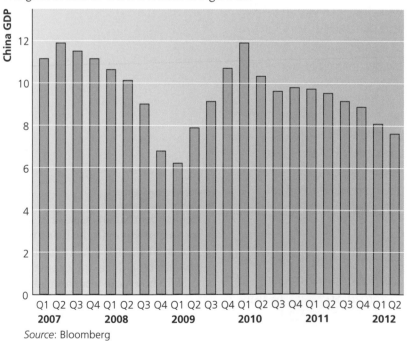
>
> *Source*: Bloomberg
>
> **Figure 8.1** China GDP: quarter compared with previous quarter (annualised % figures)

(a) Explain what was happening to the level of GDP in 2012. [4]

(b) Examine possible reasons for the change in the rate of growth rates. [12]

(c) Discuss the likely benefits of China's growth rate. [12]

Answers and quick quizzes online

Online

Examiner's summary

✔ There are two ways to measure growth: actual and potential.

✔ There are many causes of growth, and to analyse these we usually look at the forces acting on the components of aggregate demand: that is, $C + I + G + (X - M)$.

✔ The constraints on growth are many, and they depend on which country is being considered. The government might target the constraints on growth as a means of improving welfare in a country, for example by investing in new technological infrastructure.

✔ The benefits and costs of growth must be weighed against each other in your evaluation. Remember that while there may be benefits, there might be costs in both the short and long term that can cause more damage than the gains from increased income.

9 Macroeconomic objectives of governments

Current macroeconomic objectives

The six major objectives
Revised

There are six major macroeconomic objectives of governments across the world, but the priority given by each government varies, depending on its political slant.

These six objectives are:

1 Economic growth: that is, an increase in incomes or potential output.

2 Control of inflation: that is, preventing prices from rising too quickly.

3 A reduction in unemployment: the number of people available and willing to work but without employment should be ideally no more than 2%.

4 Sustainability of flows on the balance of payments: meaning that there should not be either a persistent and heavy outflow or inflow of income and wealth.

5 Making the distribution of income more equal: that is, ensuring that the top 10% slice (or decile) does not increase much faster than the bottom 10% slice.

6 Protection of the environment with its consequent impact on the various members of the global community.

Any policies adopted by governments in order to meet any one of these objectives is likely to have an impact on other objectives, and therefore governments must choose which are its most important policies. Such decisions will then determine the opportunity cost in terms of other policies or objectives.

The six objectives are outlined and evaluated below.

Objective 1: economic growth
Revised

Most countries aim to achieve growth because of the impact on incomes and jobs. We often judge the success of a government by the rate of economic growth, although there are many factors affecting economic growth that are not within the direct control of governments.

Emerging markets, including the **BRIC countries**, are seen as the drivers of the world growth in the future, with their increased incomes and efficient output. Figure 9.1 shows the **trends in growth** in selected countries in recent years.

> **Emerging markets** are countries which are currently growing and industrialising very quickly.
>
> **BRIC countries** include Brazil, Russia, India and China. These emerging economies are seen as the *building bricks* for future global prosperity.
>
> The **trend in growth** is the average rate of growth over a period of time. The trend can be shown by plotting average growth rates on a graph and drawing a line of best fit.

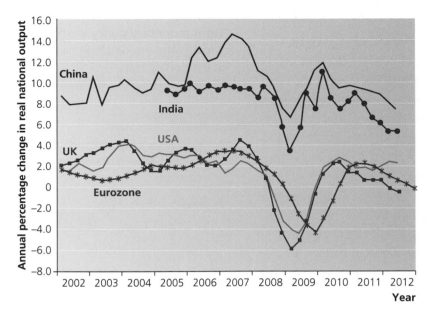

Source: Reuters

Figure 9.1 Trends in growth in selected countries. Figures above zero represent growth.

Evaluation

- From Figure 9.1 you can see that to some extent growth is out of the control of governments. All economies suffered the global recession of 2008 onwards. Many countries follow similar patterns because they are strongly interconnected through trade.

- Some economists believe that the government cannot do much to stimulate growth, and that standing back and letting markets work is the best way to control an economy.

- Developing economies such as China and India have higher growth rates than developed economies such as the UK and USA. This is in part because of **spare capacity** for growth, such as a large skilled labour force.

- The *rate of growth* is not as important as the *method of growth*, it is argued. Growth can be **jobless** if, for example growth results from investment in capital equipment which replaces workers

- Growth can have negative consequences, which we discuss on page 95. For example, carbon emissions are likely to increase which has damaging effects on environmental sustainability.

> **Spare capacity** refers to unemployed resources in an economy, which means the economy can grow quickly.
>
> **Jobless growth** occurs when an economy grows but without any increase in employment. There might also be a fall in employment if investment in machinery means that fewer workers are needed.

Objective 2: inflation Revised

Inflation is damaging to an economy for reasons including the following.

- Inflation above rates in other countries with which we trade damages our **international competitiveness** — that is, it makes our exports relatively expensive in foreign markets, and makes imports from abroad seem cheap. This tends to worsen our balance of payments.

- It is damaging for people on **fixed incomes**. If people find their incomes do not rise in **real terms** then they will get progressively worse off, even if in **nominal terms** they are earning the same amount or more.

> **International competitiveness** is the degree to which a country's goods and services can be sold on international markets.
>
> **Fixed incomes** — many groups of people, such as university students and pensioners, do not usually enjoy wage increases in line with inflation. This means that they suffer when the cost of living rises.
>
> **Real terms** are figures where inflation has been taken into account.

- High inflation rates might lead to the Monetary Policy Committee (MPC) deciding on a rise in interest rates. This is known as **tight monetary policy** and can have damaging effects, for example on investment (it falls because investment costs more).
- **Demand–pull inflation** is inflation caused by increases in **aggregate demand**, which means that spending is rising above sustainable levels. An example is that interest rates might be cut so that people want to spend more in the shops. More people wanting to buy the same amount of goods means that prices will rise.
- **Cost–push inflation** is inflation caused by decreases in **aggregate supply**, which means that costs of production are rising or firms are willing and able to produce less at any price level. For example, an increase in food prices will cause more general rises in costs in an economy.

Evaluation

Most governments see inflation as a major objective of macroeconomic policy, but there is disagreement about how important it is relative to other objectives, and how low inflation should be kept. Reasons why inflation should **not** be a major objective include:

- Inflation can be adjusted for by **index linking**. If incomes are linked to the **consumer price index**, then in **real terms**, incomes are unchanged.
- Inflation can be caused by cost increases (a decrease in aggregate supply), and cutting aggregate demand will not solve the problem. The role of the MPC is limited to controlling interest rates and quantitative easing (see page 98) but these mainly influence the demand side of the economy. They are not much use when, for example, food prices rise.
- Raising interest rates to control inflation can have damaging effects on many areas of the economy. It is argued that interest rates are a **blunt instrument** because the macroeconomic tool affects many people at the same time. There are various ways to control inflation and interest rates might be the least effective — and the most painful, some argue.
- Raising interest rates tends to increase the value of the currency. So, if the MPC raises interest rates, we would expect to see the pound getting stronger. This does relieve inflationary pressures because there is less demand for our relatively expensive exports, and imports are cheaper. But this makes our country less competitive and can cause balance of payments problems.
- If other countries which we trade with are also experiencing inflation, then the problems for international competitiveness will not occur.
- The danger of becoming 'inflation nutters', as one Bank of England governor called policy makers who devote too much of their macroeconomic powers to inflation at the expense of other things.
- A little inflation can be a good thing. It provides a cushion against deflation (falling prices).

> **Typical mistake**
>
> Many people think that the MPC has many functions and acts as part of the government. Remember that it not political and its primary function is achieving the inflation target. Other issues such as growth are of secondary importance, and are not areas for which the MPC is primarily responsible.

> **Tight monetary policy** is when interest rates are kept high because of inflationary fears.

> **Now test yourself**
>
> 1 How does a high inflation rate damage other parts of the economy?
>
> Answer on p. 106
>
> Tested

> **Index linking** is when changes in wages or pensions factor in the rate of inflation as measured by changes in a price index.
>
> When income changes are measured in **real terms**, the rate of inflation has been removed. So a 2% rise in nominal income when inflation is also 2% means that incomes are unchanged, in real terms.
>
> The **consumer price index** is the main measure of inflation used in the UK. Housing costs are not included.
>
> **Blunt instrument** — an evaluative term describing macroeconomic policies that are unable to focus clearly on one economic problem, but instead damage large areas which might otherwise have flourished.

> **Examiner's tip**
>
> In any question on the MPC make sure that you mention the inflation target.

Objective 3: unemployment

Revised

Unemployment comes in several forms (see page 66) and government policy to remove unemployment is likely to be more successful for one type of unemployment over another.

Cyclical unemployment

Cyclical unemployment or **demand deficiency** unemployment is caused by lack of spending in the economy. Here, the government may try to boost aggregate demand (government spending is a component of AD) and there will be multiplier effects.

Evaluation

- Some economists argue that the multiplier effect is very small, and the effects of government policy on the economy will be very small and will result in debts in the future.

- The little that governments can do has large time lags. By the time the policy comes into effect, the reverse is needed. For example, if the government cuts taxes to try to remove unemployment, the impact will only be felt when the economy is in recovery.

- **Classical economists** argue that the only reason that this kind of unemployment exists is because workers will not accept lower wages. They need accept that wages will be less and that they will find work.

> **Examiner's tip**
>
> Remember that cyclical unemployment occurs because of the economic cycle. There is probably nothing that governments can do to prevent the economic cycle from occurring, but the they can limit the damage of the peaks and troughs through policy decisions.

> **Demand deficiency** is where there is not enough demand for goods and services in an economy to reach the point of full employment or full capacity.
>
> **Classical economists** are the opposite of Keynesian economists. They tend to believe that there is very little unemployment if free markets are left to work for themselves.

> **Now test yourself**
>
> Tested
>
> 2 The multiplier is small when the leakages are large. What are the leakages from the circular flow?
>
> **Answer on p. 106**

Structural unemployment

Where industries are in decline there will be large pools of unemployed workers who cannot easily move into new jobs. A boost in aggregate demand by increased government spending is unlikely to help correct this problem. The coal miners, ship builders and pottery workers employed in the past will not find jobs if the government spends more on its usual activities such as education and health services. It would do better to spend on re-training workers or subsidising firms willing to take on workers to be re-trained on the job.

Evaluation

- There is an opportunity cost to subsidising firms and individuals. The money could be spent elsewhere, and raising the money means that other people have to pay more tax.

- Some people have such different skills from the ones required by employers that it will cost more time and effort to retrain workers than to give them benefits.

- Left to its own devices the economy's structural problems might well disappear over time — there are not many people training to become potters or miners in the UK today.

- If people know they will not be subsidised by the government, they might take the initiative in retraining themselves.

> **Examiner's tip**
>
> Make sure you do not confuse structural and cyclical problems. Structural problems in an economy are the problems that remain when cyclical problems have been taken into account. They occur because the way in which the country meets global demands is changing.

Frictional unemployment

Frictional unemployment occurs where people are between jobs. Here, the government can reduce unemployment by improving information flows and extending the services currently offered by job centres.

Evaluation

- If frictional unemployment is not a significant problem, then it might be better not to spend more money on this area. There is always an opportunity cost to government spending.
- Many people do not need help from the government in finding new jobs, and only a small section of the workforce and certain types of workers use the services of job centres.

Classical unemployment

Classical unemployment occurs where there are problems with the supply side of labour, e.g. the minimum wage is too high or unemployment benefits are too high. Here, the government might want to spend less rather than more, and decrease its functions in the market. We call this a 'laissez-faire' approach.

Evaluation

- Some economists such as Keynes argue that while in the classical view there is low unemployment, this is because 'in the long run we are all dead', i.e. we cannot survive while we wait for market forces to work.
- The economic cycle does suggest that much unemployment is cyclical rather than classical. This is why unemployment rises in a recession.

Objective 4: balance of payments

Revised

The objective of removing persistent **deficits** is the idea that the country should 'pay its way'. Where money is always flowing out of the country it will become poorer over time, unemployment will increase and future generations will pay the cost of over-spending today.

Evaluation

- **Surpluses** can be a problem as much as deficits. Too much money flowing into a country can be inflationary.
- A **floating exchange rate** can solve the problem. If there is a balance of payments deficit, we would expect the value of the currency to fall, making exports cheaper and imports more expensive, which in theory removes the deficit.
- A deficit on the balance of payments might be a sign that the economy is growing quickly. High incomes mean that consumers can enjoy more goods and services from abroad.
- A deficit in the balance of payments might be a sign that the economy is building up output potential for the future. For example, a country that is importing a lot of raw materials might be able to export more in the future.

> A **deficit** on the current account of the balance of payments means that more money is flowing out of the country than flowing in, in payment for goods, services, investment income and current transfers.
>
> A **surplus** on the current account of the balance of payments means that more money is flowing into the country than flowing out, in payment for goods, services, investment income and current transfers.
>
> A **floating exchange rate** is one which rises or falls in response to changes in demand and supply of a currency. It is not manipulated by a government buying or selling currencies in the market.

- Movements in goods and services are a tiny proportion of payments between countries, and capital flows for speculative or other investment purposes outweigh any problems in the 'real' economy.

Typical mistake

Speculation and other capital flows do not appear on the current account of the balance of payments, so you do not need them in the exam. However, they can be used in evaluation such as this, but you must remember that these are movements on the financial account and cannot be used to explain a **deficit on the current account**.

Objective 5: income distribution — Revised

There are several ways in which the government might try to make the distribution of income more equal:

- increasing taxes on high earners or profitable businesses
- increasing benefits to low income groups, e.g. income support or job seeker's allowance
- raising the minimum wage
- spending more money on schools and healthcare provided by the state, so that high and low income groups can enjoy similar services despite using private or state sector services

Evaluation

- Raising tax on high earners means there is less incentive to work hard, to employ more people and even to stay paying tax in this country.
- Increasing benefits might reduce incentives for people to try to go to work or to work harder for more pay.
- Raising the minimum wage can cause unemployment as firms find it hard to keep on as many workers if they have to be paid more.
- In some areas of the country, such as London, the National Minimum Wage has almost no effect because wages are above the rate because of the forces of supply and demand.
- When the government spends more on education or health there is not necessarily an improvement in standards — for example, it might mean that there are pay rises but no change in service. Money spent in some areas of the health service such as accidents and emergency will affect everyone in the same way.

Examiner's tip

Remember that raising taxes on high earners or profitable firms might not narrow income gaps. It might mean that high income earners leave the country or that there is less employment in the country as profitable firms look to employ people abroad.

Typical mistake

Raising the minimum wage does not always narrow income gaps. Remember that some people might find it harder to get a job if the national minimum wage is raised, and some might lose their jobs — although there is little evidence of this in the UK. It depends on how much the minimum wage is raised.

Examiner's tip

Remember that both rich and poor can receive benefits from spending by the government, for example government spending on roads. However, some benefits are targeted on lower income groups. For example, from 2013, child benefits will only be paid to households where no one earns more than £60,000.

Objective 6: the environment — Revised

Some main ways that governments might try to protect the environment include:

- Legislation — making laws as a county or group of countries (such as the EU) or signing up to international treaties such as Rio+20 and the Kyoto Protocol.

- Education — for example, including environmental protection in the curriculum.
- Incentives for firms and individuals — firms can receive tax breaks for cutting emissions or subsidies for using green technology.
- Involvement in market-based schemes such as the EU carbon emissions trading scheme.

Evaluation

There are many counter-arguments for governments wishing to devote a large proportion of their efforts on environment protection:

- Some people, known as 'climate change sceptics', do not accept that human activity is causing climate change.
- Alternative forms of energy, for example off-shore wind farms, are very expensive and governments have to consider the opportunity cost.
- There are other economic costs involved in protecting the environment, for example to prevent the loss of beautiful countryside.
- **Bioethanol** forces up the price of food, because it requires land which is no longer available for the production of food. This affects lower income groups proportionally more than other income groups.
- **Green taxes** (used to change peoples' behaviour regarding the environment) increase the cost of living for many people. For example, motoring costs increase, which causes cost–push inflation.
- For developing countries such as India and China, there is a moral argument — why should they adopt clean technology when the West has got very rich using dirty fuels?
- Some argue that it is much cheaper to dig coal out of the ground and burn it as the opportunity cost is very low — the coal cannot be used for anything else.

> **Examiner's tip**
>
> When you refer to the environmental aspect of government policy, always relate your answer to the people who are affected. Rather than general talk about 'the environment', economists prefer you to talk about the impact on food prices due to acid rain or flooding, or the impact on health service costs as more people are affected by exhaust fumes.

> **Bioethanol** is used as a petrol substitute for road transport vehicles. It is mainly produced by the sugar fermentation process.
>
> **Green taxes** attempt to make firms and individuals take account of the environmental impact of their market decisions. Economic incentives are given to make agents behave in a way that is environmentally sustainable. An example is a tax on landfill.

Conflicts between objectives

Conflict 1   Revised

Inflation and unemployment

When the government tries to control inflation it is likely to try to dampen aggregate demand.

- Less spending will mean less upward pressure on prices.
- The government might increase taxes or the Monetary Policy Committee might increase interest rates.
- The impact of these may well prevent inflation but they will mean less spending in the economy.
- Firms may start laying off workers because they are unable to sell all their goods and services, and as workers are laid off incomes fall and so the cycle continues.
- So, there appears to be a trade-off between the objective of controlling inflation and unemployment because in trying to control inflation, unemployment will rise.

This works in the other direction as well.

- If the government is trying to control unemployment it might start spending more on training workers or subsidising firms to take on more workers.
- This increased spending in the economy is likely to make prices in general rise.
- This is because there is more money chasing the same amount of goods and services.

The **trade-off** between these two objectives is clearly illustrated in the Phillips curve as shown in Figure 9.2. At point A there is high inflation and low unemployment, but if the government tries to move to point B it only gets rid of inflation at the expense of unemployment.

> A **trade-off** occurs when one objective is achieved at the expense of another.

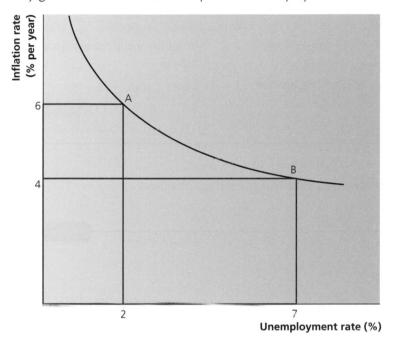

Figure 9.2 The Phillips curve

Now test yourself

3 What does the Phillips curve show?

Answer on p. 106

Tested

Conflict 2

Revised

Economic growth and sustainability

When an economy grows, standards of living tend to improve.

- For standards of living to be sustainable, growth must not occur at the expense of future generations.
- There is a conflict between enjoying a resource today and someone else enjoying it in the future.
- This is most important when considering those affected by damage to the environment when we consume resources today.
- So if our increased use of fuels means that there is more global warming then growth may not be as desirable as it first appears.
- The **six macroeconomic objectives** on page 88 must be considered.
- Governments must make a choice, weighing up the welfare of today's generation with that of tomorrow to achieve **sustainable growth**.

> **Sustainable growth** is growth that does not compromise the welfare of future generations.

Conflict 3

Inflation and equilibrium on the current account of the balance of payments

Controlling inflation should make a country more competitive internationally and therefore lead to an improvement on the balance of payments.

- Exports become relatively cheap and imports relatively expensive.

- Therefore controlling inflation should not conflict with dealing with a balance of payments deficit.

- However, the actions required to control inflation can damage the balance of payments: for example, raising interest rates to control inflation might have the effect of raising the exchange rate, which in turn makes exports expensive and imports cheap.

- By contrast, contractionary fiscal policy — which might alternatively be used to control inflation — would tend to improve the balance of payments because people will have less money in their pockets for foreign goods.

Typical mistake

Probably the most common mistake made on a Unit 2 paper is to confuse the budget with the balance of payments. Remember that a budget refers to the government's fiscal position and that the balance of payments is a record of international flows of funds.

Now test yourself

4   What is contractionary fiscal policy?

Answer on p. 106

Tested

Exam practice

Discuss the likely impact of a rise in the base rate of interest on at least two government objectives.   [30]

Answer and quick quizzes online

Online

Examiner's summary

✔ No objective can be achieved by governments without some form of impact on other objectives. There are six major economic objectives of governments, comprising control of:

  - growth
  - inflation
  - employment
  - balance of payments
  - distribution of income
  - environmental sustainability

✔ Some of these objectives are possible to achieve together, but for some there is a trade-off, i.e. more of one means less of another. You will need to be able to reason through the relationship between at least two of these six objectives.

Exam practice answers and quick quizzes at **www.hodderplus.co.uk/myrevisionnotes**

10 Macroeconomic policies of governments and conflicts

Demand-side policies

There are two demand-side policies which cause shifts in aggregate demand. They are:

- **monetary policy**
- **fiscal policy**

An increase in aggregate demand is shown by a shift to the right or up of the AD curve. The effect is to increase the price level, increase the level of real output, or both. The impact depends on the size of the multiplier and the shape and position of the aggregate supply curve.

> **Monetary policy** is the use of monetary variables such as the interest rate to achieve macroeconomic objectives.
>
> **Fiscal policy** is the stance held by government on taxation and spending; the manipulation of government spending and taxation in order to influence aggregate demand.

Now test yourself   Tested ☐

1 Why does the shape of the aggregate supply curve matter when there is a shift in aggregate demand? In your answer consider what happens if aggregate supply is

(a) horizontal

(b) vertical

(c) upward sloping (facing some bottlenecks in the economy)

Answer on p. 106

Revision activity

Sketch the effects on aggregate demand of each of the following:

- an increase in the interest rate
- a decrease in the interest rate
- an increase in taxation
- an increase in government spending

Monetary policy   Revised ☐

Monetary policy is the manipulation of monetary variables with the aim of achieving macroeconomic objectives.

- Changes in monetary variables such as the interest rate or quantitative easing have an impact on the amount of spending in the economy,
- These changes have **multiplier effects**.
- Monetary policies are determined by the **Monetary Policy Committee** (MPC) of the Bank of England.
- The main aim is to achieve the government's inflation target of a 2% increase in the consumer price index per year; other objectives of government are taken into account as secondary targets.

> The **Monetary Policy Committee** is a body set up by the government but administered by the Bank of England whose primary function is to achieve the monetary policy objective of inflation control.

Monetary Policy Committee

The government, through the **Chancellor of the Exchequer**, delegates the responsibility of monetary policy to the Monetary Policy Committee.

- The MPC is made up of nine members, five of whom work for the Bank of England including the Governor, two are academic economists and two are industrialists.
- They meet at least once a month on the first Wednesday and Thursday of each month.
- They discuss inflationary pressures that the UK economy is experiencing.
- They hear evidence from across the country about factory-gate prices, wages, unemployment, commodity prices and any other factors which might affect inflation.
- After lengthy discussion the committee votes as to whether interest rates should be raised, lowered, or kept on hold.
- In recent years, interest rate changes have only been one quarter of one per cent at a time, which allows the economy to come to terms with the decision making of the MPC.
- In 2008 much larger changes were made to try to prevent the credit crunch crisis damaging the economy too harshly.
- Members of the committee who want to be firm and cautious about inflation are known as **hawks** and they tend to want to raise interest rates, or at least not cut them very quickly. Those who are less cautious are known as **doves**. The decision made by all the hawks and doves is a fully **transparent decision** to the public because the details of voting are published soon after the meeting, so that members are accountable for their decisions and are often called to defend their views in public.

Quantitative easing

Another strand to monetary policy as exercised by the MPC is known as **quantitative easing** (QE).

- The Bank of England can make credit easier to get by issuing liquid assets — in other words, cash.
- It buys toxic, or bad, credit usually from banks.
- By 2012, £375 billion of this virtual cash had been injected into the banking system.
- QE is an important part of monetary policy because it makes more money available for banks to lend to businesses and individuals.

Time lags

Any change in monetary policy is likely to take 18 to 24 months to have its full effect because:

- Changes in interest rates do not automatically feed through to changes in people's mortgages or other kinds of loan (e.g. fixed interest rate mortgages).
- Some people's spending is not sensitive to changes in interest rates because they might not have any alternative option. They may start to borrow, but over time they may adjust their spending patterns.
- Changes in monetary variables also affect currency values, which may involve a **time lag** before any effect on export and import decisions

Typical mistake

Many students say that the government sets interest rates. This is not the case. The MPC sets rates; it is an apolitical decision maker delegated the task of reaching the government's inflation target.

The **Chancellor of the Exchequer** is the elected member of the government in charge of the Treasury, responsible for setting tax and spending, and with oversight of monetary policy, which is currently delegated to the Monetary Policy Committee.

Hawks are members of the MPC who are more likely to raise interest rates, and are more aggressive than doves in their attempts to control inflation.

Doves are members of the MPC who are less likely to raise interest rates, and are less aggressive than hawks in their attempts to control inflation.

A **transparent decision** is made when all aspects of a decision are made fully available to the public, including minutes of meetings and records of how people voted. This is an important feature of monetary policy because it improves confidence in the process of decision making.

Quantitative easing is an injection of money/liquidity into an economy by the central bank.

Typical mistake

Many students think that manipulating the interest rate is the only aspect of monetary policy. Remember that there is QE as a possibility and the UK has rolled out a £375 billion credit boost to the economy (2012 figures).

A **time lag** is the delay between the implementation of a decision and its full impact on the economy.

becomes evident; people take time to react to price changes. This may be because contracts to buy or sell are already in place at the previous price.

- Sometimes the changes in interest rates are so small that people are not very quick to react.

A rise in interest rates

A rise in the interest rate is likely to make the pound stronger against other major currencies as foreign speculators tend to buy pounds when the interest rate is higher. You can illustrate this with a microeconomic diagram showing an increase in demand as the price of currency (that is, the exchange rate) rises.

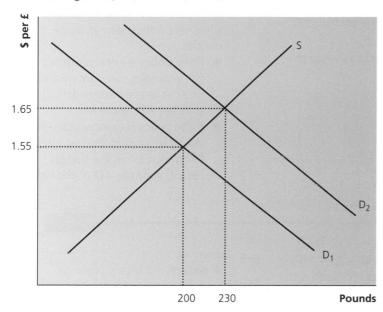

Figure 10.1 The impact of an increase in the interest rate on the exchange rate

Examiner's tip

Remember to refer to time lags as part of your evaluation of monetary policy. The delay in impact of the interest rate changes on the spending patterns in the economy helps us to assess the effectiveness of monetary policy. You would not expect the change in interest rates to have an immediate effect.

Revision activity

Go to the BBC website, visit 'News', then 'Business' and look at market data. See what has happened to major exchange rates over recent years. Has the pound recovered from its 25% fall against its major trading partners since 2007?

Now test yourself

2 What does it mean when we say the pound is stronger?

(a) Imports are more expensive.

(b) Exports are cheaper.

(c) The pound can buy more of a foreign currency.

(d) The pound is more attractive to foreign investors.

Answer on p. 106

Tested ☐

Fiscal policy

Revised ☐

Change in **taxation** and **government spending** is called fiscal policy, and it has an impact on the amount of spending in the economy.

- An increase in tax or a cut in government spending increases aggregate demand, with multiplier effects.

- An decrease in tax or a rise in government spending decreases aggregate demand, with multiplier effects.

Fiscal policy is implemented by the Chancellor of the Exchequer in the Budget, which is usually announced at the end of the financial year (March) although there have been emergency Budgets (e.g. in June after the election in May 2010) and there are mini-Budgets called the Autumn Statement which effectively allow the Chancellor to announce his or her plans for fiscal policy.

The level of spending and taxation is changed with the result that there are changes in aggregate demand.

- Fiscal or budget deficit — when the expenditure by government exceeds its taxation receipts. This causes aggregate demand to **increase.**

Taxation is the receipt of money by the government from the economy. It takes many forms, both direct (on incomes) and indirect (on spending).

Government spending is government money spent on state provision of services and goods such as health, education, income support (benefits), defence, transport and other public works schemes.

- Fiscal or budget surplus — when the expenditure by government is less than its taxation receipts. This causes aggregate demand to **decrease.**

- Expansionary or loose fiscal policy — when the government spends more than its receipts in order to stimulate the level of spending in the economy. This causes aggregate demand to **increase.**

- Contractionary or tight fiscal policy — when the government spends less than its receipts in order to dampen the level of spending in the economy. This causes aggregate demand to **decrease.**

Now test yourself   Tested ☐

3   If the government is concerned that there is too much government borrowing building up in the economy, what is the likely fiscal policy that will follow?

4   Does a Keynesian agree with the idea of tight budgets when the economy is in recession?

Answers on p. 106

Examiner's tip

Make sure that you always draw an aggregate demand curve shifting when you discuss demand-side policies.
- If the policy is contractionary (for example, raised interest rates or a cut in the budget deficit) shift the AD to the left.
- If the policy is expansionary (for example, a cut in interest rates or an increase in the budget deficit) shift the AD to the right.

Supply-side policies

The three major policies   Revised ☐

Any deliberate actions by policy makers to shift the aggregate supply curve to the right are known as **supply-side policies**. The aim is to encourage producers to produce more at any given price level. There are three major types of policy.

1   **Labour market policies.** These aim to make the workforce more cost effective and productive. The policies could range from education and training (with long-term, long-lasting impact) to cutting benefits, which may create incentives for people to get off benefits and back to work (but which may create social problems).

2   **Policies to improve competition between firms.** This might take the form of removing **patents** or making it easier for new firms to set up by relaxing regulations. In some textbooks you might see **privatisation** listed — state assets are transferred to the private sector so that they must compete on the same terms as any private firm — but there is not much scope for further privatisation in the UK.

3   **Policies to cut costs for firms.** This might include cutting taxes or reducing the National Minimum Wage (a rise in the NMW can increase costs for firms that use a lot of unskilled labour, such as in agriculture).

A **patent** is a legally binding protection for intellectual or physical ideas. They protect the holder for up to 14 years. Removing patents can stimulate production in the short term, as generic items are produced, but in the long term can result in reducing the incentive for firms to research and develop new product ideas.

Privatisation is the transfer of assets from the public to the private sector, usually through the sale of shares. It was very popular in the UK during the 1980s. It is unwise to suggest this as a future supply-side policy in the UK.

Revision activity

Sketch an aggregate supply curve shifting to the right, and make sure you add aggregate demand on your diagram. Note that there should be an increase in equilibrium real output and a fall in the average price level, although if aggregate demand crosses on the horizontal part of the aggregate supply curve there will be no change in the equilibrium output.

Examiner's tip

Make sure that you always draw an aggregate supply curve shifting to the right when you discuss supply-side policies.

Now test yourself

Tested

5   Which one of the following is a supply-side policy?
    (a) An increase in tax on firms.
    (b) An increase in the interest rate.
    (c) The introduction of a new health and safety regulation.
    (d) A cut in bureaucracy for new firms setting up.
    (e) A new tax on imports.

Answer on p. 106

Examiner's tip

Most supply-side policies have a time lag, some more than others. Spending money on pre-school education has a time lag of at least 13 years (the length of compulsory participation in schooling or training by 2015), but a policy of giving benefits to people returning to work could have immediate effects on incentives to work hard.

Conflicts between macroeconomic policies

Conflict 1

Revised

Fiscal policy and monetary policy

Changes in the planned levels of spending and taxation by the government (fiscal policy) have a direct impact on the decision making of the Monetary Policy Committee (monetary policy).

- If the MPC believes that fiscal policy is too loose (e.g. government spending is too generous relative to taxation) then the MPC might seek to counterbalance the effect on inflation by raising interest rates.

- If the MPC believes that fiscal policy is too tight (e.g. government spending is not generous relative to taxation) then the MPC might seek to counterbalance the effect on inflation by cutting interest rates.

When fiscal policy means that there is an enormous deficit, this has to be paid for by borrowing. Increased demands in the money markets for funds means that other borrowers, apart from the government, might have to pay more to borrow money. So financing fiscal policy can have an impact on market interest rates.

Now test yourself

6   Why does loose fiscal policy affect interest rates?

Answer on p. 106

Tested

Conflict 2

Revised

Monetary policy and supply-side policy

Changes in interest rates and other monetary policy decisions have a direct impact on the costs of firms, therefore shifting the aggregate supply curve.

- If interest rates rise it will cost firms more to produce, which might mean that firms are willing to produce less at any particular price level.

- If interest rates fall it will cost firms less to produce, which might mean that firms are willing to produce more at any particular price level.

Now test yourself

Tested

7   Why do firms borrow money?

Answer on p. 106

Examiner's tip

Monetary policy is not intended to influence the supply side of the economy, but this is an impact which the MPC must take into account when making its interest rate decisions.

Conflict 3

Revised

Supply-side policy and fiscal policy

Changes in most supply-side policies will have a direct impact on government spending: that is, fiscal policy. For example:

- Improving education and health services to encourage people to be more productive requires high levels of government spending.

- Increasing the length of education also means that governments will not receive money via taxes from income those students might have earned had they been at work.

In most cases:

- Supply-side policies tend to *increase* the budget deficit in the short term.

- Supply-side policies can *decrease* the budget deficit in the long term, as improved human capital means higher incomes which can be taxed by the government.

However some supply-side policies, such as reducing bureaucracy, are unlikely to make a significant impact upon **government spending and taxation** (G and T).

Some supply-side policies, such as privatisation and cutting benefits, will tend to *reduce* the budget deficit. Privatisation is a one-off benefit, and cutting benefits could increase long-term costs to the government because of the social problems involved.

> **Typical mistake**
>
> Never assume that all supply-side policies work. Many policies take years to achieve, and some might not achieve success at all. The current changes in the education system might be seen as an attempt to improve the supply side of the economy, but if some young people become alienated by the new exam system then you could argue that the supply-side policy shifts the aggregate supply curve to the left.

> **Typical mistake**
>
> Try to avoid being 'one-sided', for example when assessing supply-side policies such as cutting benefits. Remember that there are two sides to every issue and if you want to earn evaluation marks you must weigh up both sides of the argument. Evaluation is worth 25% of the marks in the Unit 2 exam.

Now test yourself

Tested

8 Why does a cut in bureaucracy improve the supply-side with no impact on the fiscal position?

9 Why do supply-side policies tend to improve human capital?

Answers on p. 106

Exam practice

(a) Using an appropriate diagram, explain what is meant by the term 'supply-side policies'. [8]

(b) Assess the use of supply-side policies as a means of addressing a problem of rising youth unemployment. [14]

Answers and quick quizzes online

Online

Examiner's summary

✔ When a macroeconomic policy is applied there will be direct effects which may or may not be seen as a successful outcome, and indirect effects, which may or may not be beneficial.

✔ The government has to prioritise the objectives that it believes are the most important at any one time, and the economist will try to predict how effective these priorities will be and what the effects of implementation will be on a wide range of variables. No economic policy comes without costs; in addition to knowing what the main macroeconomic policies are (monetary and fiscal) you also need to know the possible side effects.

Now test yourself answers

Chapter 1

1. **(a)** Land because copper is a natural resource which is included in the economic definition of land.

   (b) Enterprise because the woman has taken the risks to start a business.

   (c) Capital because the machinery is used to make other goods.

   (d) Labour because the person is working for a business.

2. **(a)** Capital good.

   (b) Consumer good.

   (c) Consumer good/service.

   (d) Capital good.

3. Correct answer is (d). The demand for specialist products makes it very difficult to increase specialisation. Specialisation is best suited to the production of mass-produced goods which enables the job to be broken down into small tasks.

4. Resources are scarce but wants are infinite, so choices must be made.

5. The holiday in Greece — this is the real cost of making a choice.

6. No resources are sacrificed in their use so the opportunity cost is zero.

7. (b) and (c) are positive statements because these can be verified by reference to data.

   (a) and (d) are normative statements because they are subjective and based on value judgements.

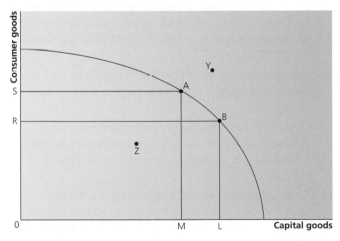

8. **(a)** At Z there will be unemployed resources because this point is not on the PPF.

   (b) Point Y is currently unattainable. It could only be achieved if there was an outward shift in the PPF.

   (c) LM capital goods.

   (d) (i) Increasing the current output of consumer goods would increase present living standards.

      (ii) However, future living standards may fall because fewer capital goods are being produced.

9. **(a)** An outward (rightward) shift because productivity would increase.

   (b) An inward shift on the PPF because productive capacity would have decreased.

   (c) This would cause an outward shift in the PPF because the extra capital would enable output per worker to increase.

   (d) This represents an increase in the working population so the PPF would shift outwards.

Chapter 2

1. Private ownership of resources; profit motive; prices are determined by the forces of supply and demand; inequality.

2. Essentially, by their purchasing decisions, consumers determine what is produced and how much.

3. Other advantages include:
   - Freedom of the individual as a consumer and as a producer.
   - Efficiency — competition provides an incentives for firms to produce as efficiently as possible.
   - Choice of goods available for consumers.
   - Innovation — profit provides an incentive for entrepreneurs to take risks and develop new products.

4. Inequality occurs because of:
   - differences in ownership of resources
   - differences in skills and qualifications of workers
   - differences in wages related to both factors influencing demand and supply of labour in different occupations

5. Other disadvantages include:
   - Possibility that monopolies will develop which could exploit consumers.
   - Unemployment and waste of resources.
   - Environmental damage because only private costs and private benefits will be considered.
   - No provision of public goods.

6. The amount demanded at given prices over a certain period of time.

7. **(a)** A rightward shift in the demand curve.

   (b) A leftward shift in the demand curve.

   (c) A rightward shift in the demand curve for houses because the substitute, rented accommodation, has increased in price.

   (d) A leftward shift in the demand curve because it has become more expensive to buy a house.

8. The amount producers are willing to offer for sale at given prices in a particular period of time.

9. **(a)** A rightward shift of the supply curve because a subsidy reduces production costs.

   (b) A leftward shift of the supply curve because higher wages would increase production costs.

   (c) A rightward shift of the supply curve because output per worker has risen.

   (d) A leftward shift of the supply curve because less tea will be available.

10 Excess supply because the quantity supplied will be greater than the quantity demanded.

11 Market forces would cause an extension of demand and a contraction in the quantity supplied, causing the price to fall to its equilibrium.

12 (a) The supply curve will shift to the left, causing a rise in the price of beef and a fall in quantity.

(b) The demand curve will shift to the right, causing a rise in price and a rise in the quantity.

(c) The supply curve will shift to the right, causing a fall in price and a rise in quantity.

(d) The demand curve will shift to the left, causing the price and quantity to fall.

Chapter 3

1 (a) PED = % change in quantity demanded/% change in price

$$= \frac{10\%}{20\%} = 0.5$$

This implies that demand is price inelastic since the result is between 0 and 1.

(b) PED = $\frac{15\%}{10\%}$ = 1.5

This implies that demand is price elastic

(c) PED = $\frac{6\%}{6\%}$ = 1

This implies that demand is unitary elastic.

2 Total revenue will increase because the price will have risen by a larger percentage than the fall in quantity demanded.

3 Demand is price elastic because the rise in price must have caused a more than proportionate fall in quantity demanded.

4 Demand is unitary elastic because the increase in price must have caused an exactly proportionate fall in the quantity demanded.

5 There are many substitutes.

6 Inelastic because for many people there are no effective substitutes and coffee forms part of their daily diet.

7 Milk is a non-durable product and part of the everyday diet of many consumers.

8 (a) +15% ÷ +10% = +1.5. Therefore tea and coffee are substitutes since the result is positive

(b) −10% ÷ +5% = −2. Therefore X and Y are complements because the result is negative.

9 (a) −9% ÷ −3% = +3. This implies that new cars are a normal good (the result is positive) and that demand is income elastic (the fall in income has led to a more than proportionate decrease in demand).

(b) −2% ÷ +5% = −0.4. Therefore soya is an inferior good because the result is negative.

(c) +2% ÷ +10% = +0.2. Therefore demand for oranges is income inelastic (the result is between 0 and +1).

10 (a) 2% ÷ 20% = 0.1. Therefore supply is inelastic since the result is between 0 and 1.

(b) 15% ÷ 5% = 3. Therefore, supply is elastic since the result is greater than +1.

11 Inelastic because tomatoes are perishable and cannot be stored and there is a long growing period.

12 It is possible that the supply of butter would be elastic if there are stocks available in refrigerated warehouses.

Chapter 4

1 The supply curve would shift to the left and become steeper.

2 If the subsidy is decreased it would cause a leftward shift in the supply curve which would cause the price to increase and quantity to fall.

3 (a) There would be a decrease in supply of engineers which would cause an increase in the wage rate.

(b) There would be an increase in demand for engineers which would cause a rise in the wage rate.

(c) This would increase the supply of engineers in the longer term, so causing a fall in the wage rate.

4 This would cause a rise in the costs of restaurants which means that the supply curve would shift to the left and they would raise their prices. How much prices rise depends on the price elasticity of demand for restaurant meals.

Waiters in restaurants would have an increase in pay if they were being paid on the National Minimum Wage. However, it could mean a reduction in the number of waiters employed.

Chapter 5

1 A market is said to fail if resources are not allocated in the most efficient way possible.

2 The social marginal cost must be equal to the social marginal benefit.

3 Only (c) and (e) would increase geographical immobility of labour; (d) would increase occupational mobility while (a) and (b) would decrease geographical mobility. In the case of (a), it would make it harder for someone to move to an area where jobs are available, while (b) would cause an increase in the cost of moving.

4 Options (a) and (d) would increase occupational mobility because they make it easier for workers to move into other occupations.

Option (b) would increase geographical mobility while option (c) would decrease occupational mobility by making it more difficult for workers to transfer into a different occupation.

5 Private goods are excludable, i.e. it is possible to prevent everyone from consuming the product, and rivalrous, i.e. consumption by one person means that less is available for others.

6 Because it is impossible to exclude people from consuming the product.

7 Use of satellite detection vans which can determine whether someone is using a television without paying for a licence.

8 (a) Private costs: raw materials, wages; cost of fertiliser to the farmer. External costs: waste discharged into river.

(b) It is difficult to place a monetary value on external costs; to quantify external costs; and the price elasticity of demand may not be known.

9 Both demand for and supply of commodities tend to be more price inelastic than for manufactured goods. Also, supply of commodities is more likely to be disrupted by extreme weather events than for manufactured goods.

10 To reduce price fluctuations of primary products.

11 When all producers are members of the buffer stock scheme; when the floor and ceiling prices are compatible with long-run supply and demand; and when members do not 'cheat' by doing deals with consuming countries.

12 No, not if the minimum guaranteed price is below the free market price.

Chapter 6

1 When an economy comes out of recession but quickly returns to another two consecutive quarters of negative economic growth. See graph below:

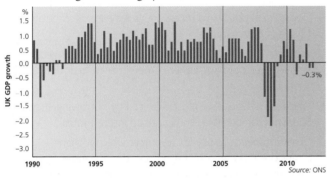

Source: ONS

UK GDP growth, quarter on previous quarter

2 It may mean that it could enjoy higher living standards, but this is not guaranteed.

3 No. If it is a one-off spike when prices go up sharply (and usually come down again) then it is neither general nor sustained. However, it could be a *cause* of inflation because when oil prices go up the cost of production rises for most firms, and this is likely to cause firms in general to raise their prices.

4 Similar items can be bought in high- and low-cost shops, so a selection of prices is gathered for each item. There are about 180 000 separate price quotations used every month in compiling the indices, covering nearly 700 representative consumer goods and services. Prices are collected in about 150 areas.

5 Reasons might include: Housing costs are excluded such as mortgage interest repayments and rent. The 650 items in the 'basket' are changed only once a year, but tastes and fashions change more quickly than this and 'special offers' temporarily change people's spending habits. For people with atypical spending patterns, such as vegetarians and non-drivers, the CPI will be unrepresentative. Quality and technology of goods change over time and this is difficult to incorporate in the measurement of CPI. For example, the quality of instant cameras has dramatically improved on a monthly basis and the basket of goods is not changed often enough to reflect this.

6 It falls by 3%.

7 It is economically inactive, e.g. students or those caring for dependants.

8 There are strict criteria for claiming JSA and many are not eligible. For example, if you refuse work that you have been offered, have a high level of savings or have a spouse with a high income you may not be eligible.

9 The Claimant Count records people who receive a financial reward for declaring themselves unemployed, whereas in the ILO method there is no reward for saying that you are unemployed. So when times are hard and there is not much money around in the economy (in a recession) the JSA tends to rise relative to the ILO. People have a stronger incentive to claim the JSA payments, are less likely to have high levels of savings or spouses with high incomes etc., which might have made them ineligible.

10 Because full-time students are not included in the official figures for employment or unemployment neither should change. However, many students do some paid work (EU students do not have any restrictions within the EU) so the level of employment might rise as casual vacancies are filled.

11 It is an import because money is flowing out of the country. Most people get confused with this because they think of themselves leaving the country as an exit not an entry. Remember to think about money flows, not the physical movement of goods or people.

12 $1 = 10 Sri Lankan rupees (LKR).

13 If actual exchange rate is $1 = 130LKR, the LKR is undervalued (cheap) and in free markets people will want to start buying from Sri Lanka until the price of Sri Lankan rupees starts to rise.

Chapter 7

1 It will rise more slowly. Government spending is an injection into the circular flow of income, so a fall in the injection means that incomes will rise less quickly than they did.

2 It will fall, with multiplier effects.

3 Initially there might be a decrease in aggregate demand as the price elasticity of demand for imports and exports tends to be low, but as time goes by you would expect aggregate demand to increase. People abroad start buying the cheaper exports and people at home stop buying the expensive imports.

4 A movement along the AD curve happens when there is a change in the price level. This might be because all costs have risen (that is, a shift in aggregate supply). A movement in AD occurs when one of the determinants of aggregate demand changes. For example, an increase in investment will increase AD. In this case there is a decrease in government spending (G) so aggregate demand decreases (shifts to the left).

5 This is the Keynesian method of drawing the AS curve. It illustrates that there can be equilibrium price level and real national output even when there is unemployment or spare capacity in the economy.

6 Interest rate increases will make loans more expensive for firms so an increase is likely to make aggregate supply fall.

7 A fall in the value of a currency makes imports expensive and exports cheap. So aggregate demand should increase. Remember to think about elasticities of demand if you want to evaluate this.

8 £2 million (2 x £1 million).

Chapter 8

1 The level of GDP has risen by 2%, whereas in the past it had risen more quickly at 3.2%.

2 An increase in investment causes aggregate demand to increase because I is a component of AD = C + I + G + (X − M). There are multiplier effects. There will also be an increase in AS because investment is an increase in capital assets, meaning there is more productive potential.

3 High exchange rates make the price of exports expensive in foreign countries, so this may stop people buying them. If exports fall, AD falls because X is a component of AD and there are multiplier effects. Likewise, if the exchange rate is high, imports are cheap and so if imports are increased, then because this is a negative component of AD then AD falls with multiplier effects. However, a high exchange rate can have the reverse effect if the price elasticity of demand for exports and imports is low.

4 The increased imports will worsen the balance of payments. If the car uses a lot of fuel, there will be increased carbon emissions, and the fuel itself will be an import.

Chapter 9

1 Distribution of income, international trade (exports become relatively expensive and imports relatively cheap) and there are adverse effects if interest rates are used to fight inflation.

2 Savings, tax and imports.

3 The Phillips curve illustrates a negative relationship between inflation (on the vertical axis) and unemployment. The implication is that if you are prepared to forgo one you can achieve success in controlling the other.

4 When government spending and taxation is used to dampen demand, perhaps by cutting government spending or raising taxation.

Chapter 10

1 **(a)** Horizontal: the increase in AD will cause an increase in output but no change in price level

   (b) Vertical: the increase in AD will cause an increase in price level but no change in real output

   (c) Upward sloping: the increase in AD will cause an increase in output and an increase in price level

2 Correct answer is (c). A stronger pound means that every pound buys more. For example, a stronger pound buys €1.25 not €1.10.

3 It is likely that it will use a tight fiscal policy, increasing tax and/or cutting spending.

4 No. A Keynesian thinks that governments should operate a loose fiscal policy in a recession, as a means of stimulating aggregate demand.

5 Correct answer is (d). Cutting bureaucracy means getting rid of regulations and other barriers that make it difficult for new firms to set up.

6 Because deficits have to be financed by borrowing. Increased demand for loanable funds puts up interest rates.

7 The firm needs to pay for resources which it then transforms into goods and services that it can sell. The time taken to transfer the resources into receipts for payment means that the firm owes people money.

8 Less bureaucracy means there are fewer rules and regulations for firms when they operate in a country. For example, it might mean that firms can take on more workers without doing full checks on their criminal records. This will cut costs for firms and mean they can increase output at a lower cost that it would otherwise be, but there are no direct payments as a result — except that those workers will start paying tax on their incomes more quickly.

9 Investment in people, such as spending on health or education, improves the productive potential of the workforce. Human assets are worth more to the economy.